AFRICA'S TURN?

AFRICA'S TURN?

Edward Miguel

Foreword by William Easterly

A Boston Review Book

THE MIT PRESS Cambridge, Mass. London, England

MIT Press books may be purchased at special quantity discounts for business or sales promotional use. For information, please e-mail special_sales@mitpress.mit.edu or write to Special Sales Department, The MIT Press, 55 Hayward Street, Cambridge, MA 02142.

This book was set in Adobe Garamond by *Boston Review* and was printed and bound in the United States of America.

Boston Review thanks the William and Flora Hewlett Foundation for supporting the publication of this book.

Library of Congress Cataloging-in-Publication Data

Miguel, Edward.
  Africa's turn? / Edward Miguel ; foreword by William Easterly.
     p. cm. — (Boston review book)
  ISBN 978-0-262-01289-8 (hardcover : alk. paper)
  1. Africa, Sub-Saharan—Economic conditions—21st century. 2. Africa, Sub-Saharan—Politics and government—21st century. 3. Political stability—Africa, Sub-Saharan—21st century. I. Title.
  HC800.M52 2009
  330.967—dc22

                                        2008051249

    10 9 8 7 6 5 4 3 2 1

For Eli

CONTENTS

William Easterly

FOREWORD

IN THE WEST, AFRICA'S IMAGE SEEMS FOREVER torn between two false extremes: Politically Correct Positive and Stereotypically Negative. Those who promote the first want to persuade us that poverty and bad government are not as bad as they seem in Africa, so a little bit of outside aid and advice can cause rapid change for the better. Those who promote the second seem happy to go along with the sensationalist media stereotypes of ubiquitous child soldiers, genocide, famine, and plague, perhaps thinking that their perspective helps make the case for more aid to Africa.

In fact, because both images are useful for aid advocacy, people often assert them together, contradictorily. Thus, a well-known Africanist who was a long-time research director at the World Bank recently made the ridiculous claim that Africa's "reality is the fourteenth century," while at the same time declaring that "change is easy." Alas, as this example shows, research and analysis of Africa has been too often polarized by advocacy agendas because, for many years, the aid agencies produced most of the Western analysis on Africa.

In the last decade, however, the monopoly of bias over analysis of aid to Africa has been broken. A new generation of academic economists has come along to look at Africa from a much more thoughtful and neutral perspective. They combine rigorous village- and household-level studies with analysis of aggregate statistics such as quantity of national rainfall and currents in economic growth. They have discarded the tortured misperceptions of Africa. They recognize positive trends—e.g. large improvements in health and education and African democratic activists kicking out kleptocrats—while not shying away from frank portrayals of the horrors of continuing wars. They work side by side with African research partners rather than patronizing them. They don't exaggerate outsiders' potential as "saviors of Africa," yet have pointed to constructive, one-step-at-a-time ways in which outsiders could support Africans in their quest for a better tomorrow.

Edward Miguel, the exemplar of clear vision and thoughtful analysis of Africa today, has been a leader of this new generation. In this marvelous book, he shows that even when progress is fragile, the case for hope in Africa is on the most solid of possible foundations: the resourcefulness and creativity of the African people themselves.

William Easterly is Professor of Economics (Joint with Africa House) and Co-director, Developerment Research Institute at New York University. His book The White Man's Burden: Why the West's Efforts to Aid the Rest Have Done so Much Ill and So Little Good *was named a 2006 Book of the Year by* The Economist.

Boston Review *wishes to express its thanks to the William and Flora Hewlett Foundation for supporting the publication of this book.*

I

Is it Africa's Turn?

THINGS WERE CERTAINLY LOOKING UP WHEN I last visited Busia, a small city in Kenya, in mid-2007. Busia, home to about 60,000 residents, spans Kenya's western border with Uganda: half the town sits on the Kenyan side and half in Uganda. As befits a border town, Busia is well endowed with gas stations, seedy bars, and hotels catering to the truckers who spend the night on the way from Nairobi to Uganda.

When I visited last June, the city was experiencing an economic renaissance. Busia's first supermarkets, ATMs, Internet cafés, and car rental businesses were all open, and residential suburbs had formed on the edge of town. The small *dukas*—shops selling home food supplies and airtime for now-omnipresent cell phones— were freshly painted with advertisements for local dairy products. And most importantly, the road from Kisumu, the economic hub of the region and Kenya's third largest city, to Busia had become a paved, two-lane highway all the way to the border, expediting trade with Uganda's productive factories and farmers.

Yet, barely a decade ago, poverty and desperation were pervasive there, as in all of western Kenya. Primary-school enrollment rates had fallen throughout the 1990s, public health surveys in 1997 showed that the HIV infection rate might be upwards of 30 percent among pregnant women, and the road into Uganda— the lifeblood of a border town and one of Kenya's critical international trade arteries—was falling apart. Long stretches of the drive from Kisumu were nearly impassable due to mooncrater potholes; cars hugged the side of the road or slalomed across the remaining patches of asphalt. Eastbound and westbound vehicles alternated control over the pavement, setting a deadly stage, especially at night, for road accidents, as oil tankers and buses sped in opposite directions.

I have visited Busia every year since 1997 to help local development-oriented nonprofit organizations design and evaluate their rural programs. In so doing, I have been exposed to impressive changes that are mirrored throughout the country. Kenyan economic growth rates surged between 2002 and 2007, achieving levels not seen since the 1970s. Last summer Nairobi's never-ending traffic jams of imported Japanese cars were but one tangible indication that Kenyans were suddenly on the move. Construction projects were everywhere, as developers took advantage of the unexpected spike in land values. New productive sectors, like same-day cut flower exports to Europe, employed tens of thousands of workers. Like a fever that had suddenly broken, the resignation and fear of the 1990s were replaced by energy, optimism, and a feeling that there was no time to lose.

But that feeling dissipated quickly in the weeks following Kenya's disputed December 27, 2007 presidential election. The incumbent president Mwai Kibaki was reelected, allegedly through heavy ballot-box rigging. The results, and subsequent violent opposition protests and ethnic clashes, surprised many Kenyans and most observers, who thought that the elections would be free and fair and that they would help Kenya turn the corner on its autocratic past. The government power-sharing deal that Kofi Annan negotiated between the government and opposition, after two months of bloodshed, has instilled tentative hope.

The recent violence in Kenya is a heartbreaking disappointment, but the Lazarus story I witnessed in Busia—though it may have been temporary—is being repeated in hundreds of cities, towns, and villages, not just in Kenya, but all over Africa. Economic growth rates are at historic highs and democratization appears finally to be taking root. Will Africa be the world's next development miracle?

IN 2000, SUB-SAHARAN AFRICA—THAT IS, all of Africa excluding North Africa, which represents only 15 percent of the continent's population—was at the end of an uninterrupted quarter century of economic and political failure, a downward tailspin that gave the world the 1984-85 Ethiopian famine, the 1994 Rwandan genocide, and more recently blood diamonds and mass amputations in Sierra Leone. Africa ranked lowest in the world in just about every economic and social indicator, including public health, as one might expect from the epicenter of the global HIV/AIDS epidemic.

Continuing the positive economic trends of the 1940s and '50s, many newly independent African countries saw improvements in the '60s. But these signs of advancement soon gave way to staggering reversals. After peaking around 1975, African per capita income steadily declined through 2000, with average living standards falling 20 percent. Kenya serves as a close stand-in for the entire continent: the timing of its economic advance and decline differs only slightly, with incomes peaking slightly later. During the same period, two other once desperately poor regions carried out an economic transformation: Indian per capita incomes doubled and Chinese levels rose four-fold.

The academic debate on what went wrong in Africa at the end of the twentieth century is extensive, but the leading culprits seem to be bad economic policy and weak state institutions. Here, though, I am more concerned with what has gone right since 2000, the turnaround in economic performance that has lifted African per capita income levels close to their all-time highs. Africa's recovery may still be modest by China's and India's standards (average annual per capita income growth for all sub-Saharan Africa has been at about 3 percent between 2000 and 2007), but it constitutes a clear break from the past, and it is now possible to wonder whether the terrible decades of war, famine, and despair are finally over. Several continent-wide trends suggest reasons to hope that they are.

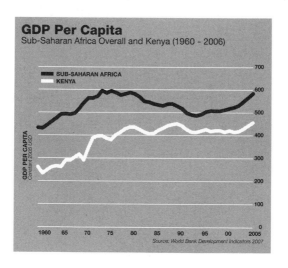

GDP Per Capita
Sub-Saharan Africa Overall and Kenya (1960 - 2006)

SUB-SAHARAN AFRICA
KENYA

GDP PER CAPITA
Constant 2005 USD

700
600
500
400
300
200
100
0

1960 65 70 75 80 85 90 95 00 2005

Source: World Bank Development Indicators 2007

SUB-SAHARAN AFRICA HAS BECOME MUCH more democratic since 1991, and this change has brought new faces into power and challenged old ways of doing business in the halls of government. Although Kenya's recent stolen election was a huge step backwards, there was a time not long ago when opposition parties were not even allowed to contest African elections, and all private media outlets were banned.

Freedom House, an independent nonprofit organization, produces a commonly used index of democratic freedoms, assigning values from one (most democratic) to seven (least). In the 1970s and '80s most countries in Africa averaged democracy scores hovering around six, a level at which political freedoms are basically nonexistent, dissident speech is violently repressed, and elections—if they are even held—are mainly for show.

Starting in 1991, however, citizens in dozens of African countries fought for political change. Some were inspired by the freedom

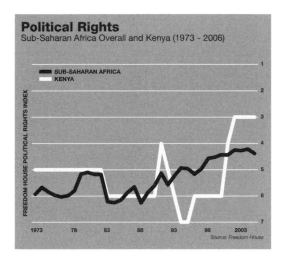

Political Rights
Sub-Saharan Africa Overall and Kenya (1973 - 2006)

SUB-SAHARAN AFRICA
KENYA

FREEDOM HOUSE POLITICAL RIGHTS INDEX

1
2
3
4
5
6
7

1973   78   83   88   93   98   2003

Source: Freedom House

wave then sweeping the Soviet Bloc and the de-
mise of apartheid in South Africa. By 2007 the
African Freedom House average had jumped
to a four. Thus, the typical African country
is still not as democratic as Sweden or India,
but progress has been widespread and visible.
Opposition parties are ubiquitous and open
debate the norm in a growing number of African countries, putting them far ahead of the

entrenched dictatorships in Asian economic stars like China and Vietnam in terms of developing free political institutions.

Until its recent relapse, Kenya had experienced an even more inspiring turnaround, from a Freedom House ranking of seven in 1995 to a three following the 2002 elections won by then-opposition leader Kibaki. Daniel arap Moi, a member of the Kalenjin ethnic group and a violent, polarizing, and autocratic ruler who became president in 1978, imprisoned and tortured hundreds of dissidents when he officially turned the country into a one-party state in the 1980s. By the 1990s Kenya's political institutions were every bit as corroded as the Kisumu-Busia highway.

Popular protests—buttressed by foreign donor pressure—forced Moi to hold Kenya's first competitive elections in a generation in 1992 and again in 1997. But neither election was fair; Moi held all the levers of state power and would never allow himself to lose. Ethnic clashes—most likely manufactured by the president himself—broke out before both polls and served to intimidate the opposition, which was already reeling from the blatantly pro-government electoral commission and biased state TV coverage. As the government looked the other way, tens of thousands of Kikuyu families were driven off their land in the Rift Valley by Kalenjin youth militias, which saw (and continue to see) the Rift Valley as Kalenjins' ancestral homeland and birthright.

Kenya held another national election in 2007. But this time the political opposition—led by long-time dissident Raila Odinga, himself imprisoned for over eight years without trial and tortured by Moi—was leading opinion polls over the now-incumbent Kibaki, who came to power when Moi finally stepped down. Political coverage in flourishing independent newspapers, on radio, television, and the Internet was exhilarating and no-holds-barred. Peaceful protests were ubiquitous. As the incumbent party faced probable defeat in a second consecutive election, Kenya was starting to look like a real democracy.

But things did not work out the way they were supposed to. After Odinga moved ahead in the early election returns, Kenya's Electoral Commission delayed vote counting for two days before producing vote tallies that unexpectedly put President Kibaki in the lead. Many international observers, and even the Commission's own head, claimed rigging was the cause: in some of Kibaki's Kikuyu strongholds, the president received tens of thousands more votes than the total number of registered voters.

The result was massive opposition protests that were suppressed, often violently, by police. The post-election anger also provided a political opening for renewed Kalenjin-Kikuyu clashes in the multiethnic Rift Valley, the products of a dispute that had largely been on ice since the mid-1990s but was never settled. Hundreds of thousands of Kenyans of all ethnic groups, but disproportionately Kikuyus, were driven out of their homes after the election. A country lauded globally for hosting its troubled neighbors' refugees—from Ethiopia, Somalia, Sudan, and Uganda—suddenly had its own refugee camps. Kenya's success was apparently far more fragile than it had seemed even days earlier.

While its Freedom House rating is sure to worsen following the rigged election, some of Kenya's recent democratic gains remain robust, as evidenced by the boisterous new opposition media that openly challenged the results, the mass opposition rallies, and the fact that Odinga's opposition party, despite losing the presidency, did manage to win control of parliament and force Kibaki to share power. These changes have been sustained by increasingly bold Kenyan civil-society leaders, journalists, and anti-corruption campaigners, including Nobel Peace Prize–winner Wangari Maathai, who will not allow a return to one-party rule.

Are Africa's democratic reforms a partial explanation for its encouraging recent economic performance? Economist Amartya Sen has famously described how democracy improved the Indian government's economic policies and, in particular, its response to famines. Although it is impossible to prove a causal link, there are good conceptual reasons to believe that democracy sometimes plays midwife to economic rebirth. Democratic elections force politicians to be more receptive to voters' needs: a free press means government policies are scrutinized and malfeasance investigated, and elections provide discipline for even the most venal or incompetent politicians. Get caught stealing and you are unlikely to return to a plum MP post. Africa's recent progress in both political freedom and economic growth could well be connected.

As important as Africa's internal political and social changes may be, global economic conditions have also been critical, and in recent years nothing has been more salient than China's rise as an economic force.

China's miracle—from rice paddies to mag-lev trains in one generation—affects Africa in multiple ways. The first is through international trade. Total Asia-Africa trade increased to more than $100 billion dollars in 2006 from trivial levels a decade earlier, and China has been partner to much of that gain. Rising commodity prices are a big part of the story. Global prices for petroleum, minerals, and agricultural products have soared over the past five years as surging Asian demand meets limited world supplies.

Crude oil is the best-known example. Its price has more than tripled since 2000, depositing many more dollars in the coffers of the big African producers like Nigeria, Angola, Chad, Sudan, and Gabon. The petroleum for Asian factories and urban commuters has to come from somewhere, and Africa is filling the gaps.

But oil is not Africa's only significant export. The per-unit price of copper soared from about $70 to $350 between June 2001 and June 2007, a boon to Zambia, Africa's largest producer. Kenya and its East African neighbors have benefited from coffee's rise. Prices have been frothy, jumping from $41 per unit in 2001 to $113 in 2007. This increase puts more money in the pockets of coffee farmers, many of whom are smallholders. The consensus is that hungry Chinese consumers are behind a big chunk of all these rising prices.

Gains in key export sectors sometimes help people who are not growing coffee or mining copper themselves. For instance, Kenya's Busia is not a coffee-producing region, but it still benefits from higher coffee prices. As coffee producers in central Kenya get richer, they buy more of Busia's fish and plantains, and also more Ugandan goods, sending ever more trucks (and truckers) laden with imports through the border city.

While rising demand for commodities is one way that Asia's economic boom helps to raise African living standards, China's economic involvement in Africa now goes far beyond arms-length imports and exports. Chinese firms have begun investing directly in African oil and mineral producers and in roads, dams, and telecommunications infrastructure. It is estimated that annual Chinese direct investment in Africa surpassed the one billion dollar mark in 2005 and has continued to rise since. Shuttered factories and mines have been brought back to life and severed roads restored. The spread of cell phone technology has allowed rural African grain markets to function more efficiently, probably improving the lives of consumers, farmers, and traders alike.

No one knows the exact figures, but hundreds of thousands of Chinese workers and entrepreneurs have also migrated to Africa in search of their fortunes. This new Afro-Chinese community—from telecom engineers to owners of small Asian restaurants and medicine shops—has been a striking new presence in my own recent travels in both West and East Africa.

Why have Chinese individuals and firms dived in when European and U.S. investors have largely shied away? In discussions with Chinese investors, it seems the key motive is simple: profit. Africa provides bountiful profit opportunities across multiple economic sectors for Chinese firms flush with cash from their boundless growth at home. Chinese investors also have a major advantage over their Western counterparts in that they know how to make money in a developing-country business environment where the rule of law is optional, corruption and bribery are the norm, and infrastructure is patchy. Their experiences at home give them a big leg up on the competition.

But the importing of Chinese business practices along with Chinese direct investment is not wholly positive for Africa. Take the example of Zambia's decrepit Chambishi mine, bought out by a Chinese state-owned enterprise and reopened in 2003 to great fanfare. Local support for the project quickly evaporated when brutal labor conditions came to light: workers were given inadequate safety equipment, paid below the national minimum wage, and denied days off—working conditions similar to what many Chinese mine workers face. Perhaps in part due to disregard for worker safety, more than fifty workers died in a serious 2005 accident that shut down the Zambian mine.

A U.S. or U.K. firm with such an appalling safety record would probably face investigations, protests, or even boycotts back home, and the bad PR would likely push it to improve working conditions. Recall the uproar when awful conditions in Nike's Asian factories came to light. But Chinese firms are not subject to the same scrutiny as their Western counterparts with respect to worker, environmental, and human rights issues. The repressive political environment in the People's Republic ensures that Chinese firms never have to say they're sorry, and they thus have a far freer hand than Westerners to squeeze profits out of African workers. While the Chambishi copper mine eventually reopened, the belief that Chinese investment brings slave-labor conditions remains widespread in Zambia. Some have begun to ask whether Chinese investment is worse than no foreign investment at all, as it seems increasingly out of step with Africans' democratic aspirations.

Even more controversially, Chinese investors have taken the lead tapping into Sudan's rich crude oil reserves. Western energy firms have shunned the Khartoum regime as punishment for its support for the *janjaweed* militias that have massacred thousands of civilians in Darfur and displaced millions more. This has left the oil playing field to the Chinese alone, and they have responded by supplying the Sudanese government critical military assistance and diplomatic support at the United Nations. Ironically, Western sanctions have only strengthened China's bargaining position vis-a-vis Khartoum by eliminating potential competition, boosting their profits.

Sudan is not the only oil producer receiving no-strings-attached Chinese investment and aid. Angola and Chad are two other recipients with questionable human rights credentials and some of the world's worst corruption. Given these countries' unscrupulous leaders and repressive politics, it is unclear whether expanded oil production will yield higher living standards any time soon.

Leaving controversial cases like these aside for the moment, China's economic rise has clearly benefited many millions of Africans, especially through growing trade and higher global commodity prices. And the billions in Chinese investment currently pouring into Africa hold out the possibility of better infrastructure and industrial development in the long run: in 2007, China committed another $20 billion to finance trade and infrastructure development throughout Africa.

Beyond the rise of China, access to rich-country markets for agricultural exports is a key issue for African economies. In the past, the United States, European Union, and Japan have forcibly opened foreign markets to "free trade" in sectors where those wealthy economies have the competitive edge, while subsidizing their own inefficient farmers with hundreds of billions of dollars each year and using tariffs and quotas to keep foreign agriculture off our dinner tables. This is one of the most hypocritical of all international trade injustices but also one that seems impervious to reform efforts.

Cotton is an extreme example of how rich-country policies hinder African economic development. In recent years, 25,000 U.S. cotton farmers have received more than $3 billion a year in government subsidies. The resulting surge in U.S. production floods global markets and drives down world cotton prices, hurting millions of poor cotton farmers in Benin, Burkina Faso, Mali, and Tanzania, for whom higher cotton prices would improve living standards. If U.S. policymakers are genuinely interested in keeping Africa's current economic turnaround going, reducing agricultural subsidies to our domestic cotton farmers would be an obvious starting point.

Recent history suggests that unilateral trade liberalization by rich countries can make a difference. In 2000 the United States enacted the African Growth and Opportunity Act (AGOA), which reduced tariff rates and lifted quotas on African textiles. It is credited with spurring textile production in a few African countries, including Kenya. A broader opening of rich country markets could have even more profound benefits. Yet here China's growing economy creates tough competition for Africa. The 2005 expiration of the Multi-Fiber Agreement, which ended most textile and apparel quotas worldwide, allowed China's low-cost factories to compete freely with other textile producers for the first time, and China's share of rich-country markets has surged. Africa's textile producers have been among the main losers, and many of AGOA's initial gains have eroded.

The noncompetitiveness of African textiles is emblematic of a broader failure of the recent economic expansion. While natural resource and some agricultural exports have grown, industrial transformation is not driving Africa's growth: in most African countries, the manufacturing sector remains as small today as it was in 2000.

THE ROLE OF FOREIGN AID IS ONE OF THE most contentious issues in development economics today. Champions of foreign aid like Jeffrey Sachs of Columbia University claim that dramatically boosting foreign aid is *the* key to breaking poor regions like sub-Saharan

Africa out of their "poverty traps," situations in which countries' own poverty prevents them from bootstrapping their way to a better future. Sachs' position is that a large aid infusion will provide poor Africans with enough spare cash to save, invest, and finally grow on their own.

Opponents of increased foreign aid, led by William Easterly at NYU, point to the fact that Africa remains desperately poor today despite the hundreds of billions of dollars of aid that have already been routed there. In other words, if there really was a poverty trap, the foreign aid already donated provided ample opportunity for Africans to break themselves out of it.

Many social science researchers have sought to establish foreign aid's causal impacts on economic growth, but there are still no definitive statistical answers. Yet a look at the raw data on foreign aid across regions and time suggests that aid has probably played a rather small role in Africa's recent economic success.

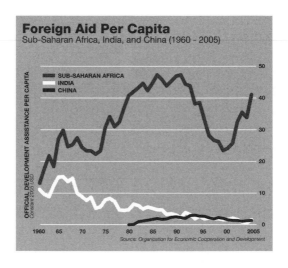

Foreign Aid Per Capita
Sub-Saharan Africa, India, and China (1960 - 2005)

SUB-SAHARAN AFRICA
INDIA
CHINA

OFFICIAL DEVELOPMENT ASSISTANCE PER CAPITA
Constant 2005 USD

1960   65   70   75   80   85   90   95   00   2005

Source: Organization for Economic Cooperation and Development

The first instructive comparison is Africa versus the world's two other poor giants, China and India, both of which were at African per capita income levels in the 1970s. It is striking how high foreign aid to Africa currently is in per capita terms: overseas development assistance is a full order of magnitude higher in Africa than in China or India, as it was during the critical 1980-2000 period when those Asian countries moved forward economically and Africa declined. It seems clear that foreign aid is not necessary for economic development.

Another issue is that foreign aid to Africa increased in the 1980s precisely when its economies started to collapse. You might wonder if foreign aid caused the collapse, but that probably would be inaccurate. Increased foreign aid flows could have been a response to the deteriorating economic circumstances. But this sort of concern makes it very difficult to understand foreign aid's impact. Foreign aid can affect economic growth but it also reacts to local economic conditions, and disentangling causes and effects in the statistics is hard.

A more promising way to get analytical leverage is to compare African economic growth in the 1980s to that in the 1990s. At the tail end of the Cold War, levels of foreign aid to Africa were at historical highs, as the United States and the Soviet Union each plied countries with cash to win their diplomatic support in that grand struggle. Yet foreign aid to Africa fell off a cliff—by nearly 50 percent—between 1990 and 1995, when African countries lost their geopolitical significance. What was the impact of this sudden change, driven mainly by external political factors rather than in reaction to internal economic performance, on African economies? You could think of this kind of sharp, unexpected change as a natural experiment.

A close look at trends in African GDP per capita indicates that average African economic performance remained pretty much the same throughout the 1990s—stable stagnation, if you like—despite the sudden aid drop off. Once again it does not appear that we should look to foreign aid to explain the key turning points in African economic growth performance.

These patterns certainly do not mean that all foreign aid is useless. There are many aspects of human well-being—in education and healthcare, for instance—that are affected by foreign aid but do not show up in short-run national income figures. The recent international campaign to fund anti-retroviral drugs is a dramatic example, and it has already saved thousands of African lives. Foreign aid can sometimes improve lives today without changing the bottom line or stimulating the economy as a whole. However, the lack of correspondence between aid and growth should make us more skeptical about simplistic claims that boosting foreign aid alone will break Africa out of its persistent poverty and lead to sustained economic progress. Healthy skepticism about foreign aid's benefits is particularly appropriate in countries where corruption remains widespread and much of whatever aid does arrive will be squandered.

VIOLENCE LIES JUST BELOW THE SURFACE of politics in poor countries and can derail economic gains. As Kenya illustrates, sub-Saharan Africa is no exception. In fact, African countries have suffered the greatest number of armed conflicts in the world over the past three decades: 70 percent have experienced at least one year of armed conflict since 1980. The damage tends to spill over into neighboring countries. Kenya's January 2008 political turmoil shut down the Kisumu-Busia highway, temporarily cutting off oil supplies into Uganda.

The past few years have seen some optimistic trends on the conflict front, but overall it is a mixed bag. The good news is that several of the most stubborn civil wars—including those in Angola, Liberia, and Sierra Leone—have finally come to an end since 2000, and the conflict in northern Uganda is moving toward resolution. Post-apartheid South Africa has avoided a political explosion, at least for the time being.

And the postwar recoveries in many African countries such as Mozambique and Uganda show that some economies can quickly overcome the toxic legacies of armed strife. In the cases of Sierra Leone and Uganda, there are signs that the civil war has not permanently demoralized survivors. In fact, experiencing conflict's horrors seems to give some people the will to strive for a better society. Chris Blattman's field research among former Ugandan child soldiers finds that those abducted by the rebels are actually more politically engaged today than those who escaped, while my work with John Bellows shows that members of Sierra Leonean households that suffered violence are more likely to vote, participate in community meetings, and contribute to local school projects than their neighbors who were spared direct violence. These findings highlight the incredible resilience of African households.

Despite these success stories, the total proportion of African countries engaged in ongoing armed conflicts has not budged, remaining near 30 percent since 1995, as new conflicts, such as Côte d'Ivoire's, take the place of the old ones, and old conflicts restart (Niger).

The gravest threats, in my view, are the armed conflicts in Congo and Sudan, Africa's largest countries, bordering a combined total of fifteen other nations. African civil wars also have a history of eclipsing national frontiers: the Liberian civil war led to Sierra Leone's conflict, the Rwandan genocide provided the spark for Congo's current mess, and Sudan's Darfur conflict has already rekindled Chad's long-simmering civil war. Unless the wars in Congo and Sudan end, they will soon threaten Africa's new democracies and economic success stories.

There is growing evidence that African civil violence can be precipitated by adverse economic conditions, and in particular by sharp drops in national income. Of course, this is not always the case: Kenya's crisis broke out during good economic times. But more often than not, extreme poverty breeds desperation and makes taking part in organized violence or crime more attractive. Exploiting two different natural experiments, researchers find that external factors that hurt African economies can set off armed conflict. Large drops in rainfall levels—which lead to economic collapse in agrarian societies—and reductions in key commodity prices have both been linked to the outbreak of civil conflict.

If the economic growth of the last seven years continues for another decade or two, African countries will be considerably richer and more diversified and thus at less risk of falling into conflict. But in the meantime, sudden economic shocks linked to weather or commodity prices are a tremendous risk factor.

Rather than waiting until conflicts arise, we might target foreign aid to vulnerable countries beforehand. I call this attempt to bolster fragile states in their most trying years, "rapid conflict prevention support" or RCPS. Tracking current rainfall levels and commodity price movements is a good way to figure out which countries should receive the aid. The hope is that using more of the existing

foreign aid pool as *insurance* for the poorest
African countries in this way could pay off
by preventing armed conflicts that jeopardize
whole regions. I do not think RCPS insurance
should (or could) entirely replace traditional
aid focused on infrastructure, health, or education. But given that the fruits of so much
foreign assistance are currently destroyed by
armed conflict, or diverted to humanitar-
ian relief after wars have already broken out,
RCPS is a natural complement to standard
foreign assistance.

An existing program that provides drought
assistance to farmers in Botswana shows that
an RCPS insurance mechanism can work.
Drought is a frequent visitor to Botswana,
as in much of the semiarid tropics. Starting
in the 1970s, the government implemented
the groundbreaking Drought Relief Program
(DRP) to help its people cope through dry
periods. The DRP consists of direct income
support for rural households in these years,

including both public works employment and food aid for the most vulnerable farmers.

It is estimated that up to 60 percent of rural Botswanans received some DRP assistance during the country's severe mid-1980s drought. (To put that in perspective, Medicaid, the largest U.S. social program providing health care for poor families, covers only 13 percent of the population.) In those difficult years, DRP helped preserve social stability by keeping rural poverty and income inequality in check.

But Botswana's government probably got its money's worth: the country has not had a single year of armed conflict since independence in the 1960s. Botswana has been Africa's economic superstar for the past forty years, and former Botswana president Quett Masire has claimed that the drought insurance played an important role in its success. This agricultural insurance program is part of the social contract between the people of Botswana and their democratically elected government. It helps maintain peace and prosperity in one small corner of sub-Saharan Africa. Other African countries at risk of drought could benefit by following in Botswana's footsteps with similar programs.

UNFORTUNATELY, THE RISK OF DROUGHT might be increasing. Half a world away, China's manufacturing boom may as well be on another planet but for one thing: the lives of African peasant farmers and Chinese factory workers—and everyone else on the globe—are connected by our collective effect on Earth's climate. For poor African farmers, weather determines whether the next harvest will yield enough food to eat. What comes out of factory smokestacks in China could literally be a matter of life and death if changing global weather means less rain for Africa, leading to poverty and war.

China's modern economic growth is fuelled by burning coal, gas, and oil. Between 2002 and 2004, energy use in China increased by a staggering 33 percent, and China became the world's biggest greenhouse-gas polluter in 2007. Together, China and the United States account for over 40 percent of global CO_2 emissions, the main culprit behind global warming.

The most recent UN report predicts that temperatures worldwide will increase anywhere from 2.0°F to 11.5°F (1.1°C to 6.4°C) during the twenty-first century. While this rise in temperatures will have a major impact on agriculture, for those of us living in advanced, post-industrial—and air-conditioned—societies like the United States, what do higher temperatures really mean? Perhaps a slightly bigger electric bill at the end of each summer month (counterbalanced with smaller heating bills in winter). Some parts of the United States may be buffeted by stronger hurricanes and tornadoes, but climate change in this range won't be catastrophic for most rich countries. Silicon Valley's idea factories and New York's investment banks will keep on humming even if it is a few degrees warmer outside.

But not so for Sudan, Chad, or their neighbors. Several leading international climate scientists predict that conditions will get worse in Africa's Sahel, a parched stretch of earth containing Chad and Niger, as well as parts of Sudan, Mali, Senegal, and their neighbors. The Sahel is home to over one hundred million of the world's poorest people. Average annual per capita income in the fifteen Sahelian countries is only $346, and the entire region is racked by political instability and warfare. Princeton University's Geophysical Fluid Dynamics Laboratory (GFDL) has developed a climate model that offers dire forecasts, predicting that average temperatures in the Sahel could rise 6.3°F (3.5°C) and rainfall could drop by 24 percent over the next eighty years. So there will be less rain and what little does fall will evaporate more quickly due to higher temperatures. One of the driest places on earth may get even drier.

If its fragile soils turn into desert sand, the region's economic situation could grow worse. It is the cruelest of ironies that the poorest people in the world—in the region least able to deal with extreme weather—could be the biggest losers in the global climate change lottery.

Not all climate models produce the same bleak forecasts as that of the GFDL researchers. But given the potentially disastrous consequences for the people of the Sahel, it is worth planning for the worst through new aid policies like RCPS, as well as more research into drought-resistant crop varieties suited to the region.

Looking back at Africa's first four decades of independence, it seems that everyone—including Africans themselves—were far too optimistic about how their economic and political fortunes would play out.

With a few notable exceptions (such as Ethiopia), African nations were inventions of the colonial powers, lines on maps with little real historical or social meaning. (Does "the Central African Republic" sound to you like a name people chose for themselves to express their national identity, or one imposed by a colonial bureaucrat?) Colonizers placed strict limitations on African political participation prior to independence, which impeded the development of genuine local politics. A few African countries, like Ghana, had strong independence movements, but in most cases, especially in Francophone Africa, independence simply dropped into people's laps.

It should not be surprising that it is taking a full generation or more for real nationhood to take root in these infant countries. Everything started from scratch after independence. Politicians had to figure out how to forge political compromises across class, regional, gender, linguistic, tribal, and religious lines. History and civics textbooks needed to be written. Citizens had to come up with their own national narratives and heroes. In Kenya leaders had to deal with the toxic legacy of the Mau Mau uprising, which became a civil war pitting Kikuyu neighbors against one other.

Creating new identities and institutions is not something that foreign colonizers, aid donors, or the IMF and World Bank are willing or able to do. That kind of transformation demands visionary leaders, who have too often been lacking in Africa, or have themselves been victims of political violence. Further complicating matters, leaders and citizens trying to assemble structures of civic life must contend with the immediate economic imperatives of boosting agricultural productivity, educating the workforce, and building a modern transportation infrastructure.

Historically, the process of creating viable nations has been costly in time and blood. The closest parallel to Africa's painful post-colonial transition is probably Latin America's trajectory after its independence from Spain and Portugal in the 1810s and 1820s. Like twentieth-century Africa, the newly free Latin American republics suffered many decades of civil and international wars, economic stagnation, and political repression before finally establishing stronger states in the late 1800s. These nineteenth century Latin American conflicts were as devastating as the worst African wars, if not more so: in the 1864-1870 War of the Triple Alliance, Argentine, Brazilian, and Uruguayan troops killed over half the prewar population of Paraguay, as they snatched chunks of its land. The comparison with the Democratic Republic of Congo's ongoing conflict—which has lured troops from at least five of its neighbors, all grabbing at Congo's mineral trove and leaving millions of civilians dead—is irresistible.

Nation-building has never happened overnight, and that includes the United States. Our own brutal civil war took place eighty years after independence from Britain, and it was not until after that transformative war that the

United States became a genuine economic and military power. After its forced opening to the outside world in 1853, Japan suffered three decades of political instability and economic stagnation before it too found its institutional footing and started on its unprecedented path of economic development.

FOR THE FIRST TIME IN A LONG WHILE, there is genuine hope today that Africa is on the path to real economic and political progress, and may finally catch up to the rest of the world economy. International trade is rising, better roads and new technologies like cell phones are improving millions of lives, and more countries than ever are turning to democracy. The economic boom and political opening I witnessed in Kenya shows what is possible.

Unfortunately, the latest Kenyan crisis also reinforces the point that Africa is not yet over the hump. The fact that post-election violence could engulf East Africa's richest and most democratic country overnight—and so readily threaten the past decade's strides—highlights how fragile its gains really were. Kenya is one country out of more than forty in sub-Saharan Africa, so it would not be right to over-interpret events there. But sadly, Kenya is not alone: Côte d'Ivoire and Zimbabwe, two of Africa's most prosperous and stable countries in the early 1990s, have also imploded in bloody political conflict. Other African countries, too, may be just one contested election, one drought year, one plummeting commodity price, or a global economic recession away from similar meltdowns.

It is still too early to know if Africa's time is now. In the meantime, international efforts to reduce Western farm subsidies, use foreign aid as insurance against conflict risk in the most vulnerable countries, end the wars in Darfur and Congo, and promote agricultural adaptation to climate change are concrete steps that may help solidify Africa's nascent transformation.

II
Forum

Robert H. Bates

IN 1997 THE AFRICA ECONOMIC RESEARCH Consortium—a network of professional economists headquartered in Nairobi and ramifying throughout Africa—launched a study of the continent's economic performance in the post-independence period. In 2007, it published the two-volume product of this effort, *The Political Economy of Economic Growth in Africa, 1960 - 2000*. Among its many findings is one highly relevant here: an understanding of the economics of Africa requires an understanding of its politics. I participated in the project, and as it was coming to an end, I asked myself, "Were we now to address Africa in the period since the year 2000, would we find it much changed?"

The answer was a resounding, "Yes!" In his essay, Edward Miguel highlights several reasons why.

Since the mid-1990s, the economies of Africa have grown, and all who experienced the misery of the collapses of the 1970s will rejoice at this. Peace has returned in Liberia, Rwanda, and Sierra Leone; all will celebrate this change as well. Governments in Africa now periodically contest elections. As Miguel suggests, for the first time in decades, Africa appears to enjoy the prospects of prosperity, peace, and good governance.

But Miguel overlooks some reasons for Africa's new prosperity. And I am more skeptical than he concerning the stability of Africa's politics and the quality of its governance.

Miguel rightly notes the impact of economic growth in India and China on Africa's economies. He fails, however, to stress three other factors.

One is the re-integration of South Africa—and its economy—into the African continent.

With the fall of apartheid came a surge of private capital northward as South African firms invested in commerce, brewing, mining, and banking elsewhere in Africa.

Africa's emigrants have also contributed to the growth of its economies. The collapse of Africa's economies in the 1970s and 1980s led to the flight of citizens abroad. The subsequent flow of funds from these expatriates now contributes to the continent's prosperity. Visitors to Ghana, for example, soon learn that the construction in newer suburbs of Accra has, to a great degree, been financed by Ghanaians abroad. Remittances rank as the country's second largest source of foreign earnings, less than the gains from gold exports, but greater than those from cocoa.

I would also draw attention to a third economic change: the movement of the petroleum frontier from the Middle East to West Africa. Africa's established oil regimes—Gabon, Angola, Cameroon, and Nigeria—have been joined by the smaller states that dot its western coastline. The United States already imports one-quarter of its petroleum from the region. As more of the West African oil fields come into production, this fraction will rise. Increasing exports of oil yield major increases in export earnings for the economies of Africa.

While significant economically, each of these changes is fraught with additional implications. Reflect on the rise of India and China, for example. Viewed in historical perspective, imperialism in Africa endured but a moment. For eons, East Africa looked eastward toward the Indian Ocean rather than northward toward Europe. Might not the re-entry of Asia on the African scene represent a return to a "natural" configuration, in which Kenya, Tanzania, or Mozambique turn first to India and China and only then to London or Paris when negotiating their futures? Reflect, too, on the emergence of Africa's oil economies. Where oil appears, there arrive the armed forces of the industrial states. In response to the increase in oil production in West Africa, the United States is now extending its military reach to the region. Both the growth of Asia and the increase in petroleum exports have sparked the renewal of economic growth in Africa. But they also limn a new geopolitical order.

As we consider the myriad effects of increasing African ties to Asia, it is vital to remember that economic improvement in Africa can be fleeting. Côte d'Ivoire and Kenya were once regarded as examples of successful development in Africa. One now stands divided, with different zones occupied by different political forces, and the other is teetering on civil war. Both underscore the fragility of peace and prosperity in Africa. That the major portion of Africa's wealth is lodged within such fragile political entities as Nigeria and South Africa does not bode well for the future welfare of the continent. Half the wealth of Africa accrues to those two states. The last national elections in

Nigeria were stolen and the current president continues to rule only because the courts allow him to, fearing the chaos that a new election would bring. And in South Africa, the ruling party's choice of Jacob Zuma as its candidate for president—poorly educated, populist, and indicted for corruption—will surely raise fears that could stifle the growth of the economy.

As Miguel notes, peace *has* returned to some of the most violent parts of Africa. But conflict still characterizes much of East and Central Africa and it has broken out afresh in the Sahelian zones. Miguel also points out that the majority of governments in Africa are chosen in competitive elections. But, as events in Nigeria reveal, incumbents have learned how elections can be managed; party competition does not imply political accountability. The tragic consequences of Kenya's last election provide further evidence that, when faced with the threat of loss of office, incumbents are willing to turn from peaceful competition to political violence.

So, yes, things have changed. However, I would describe the change as one of magnitude rather than character. There is economic growth, but much of it derives from primary products. The structures of Africa's economies remain unaltered. Several of the most intense conflicts have ended, but others continue and new ones threaten to break out. Political competition has replaced authoritarian governments, but governments have learned to rig elections so as to retain power. While I join Miguel in celebrating the progress that is being made, my joy is much more tempered.

Ken Banks

EDWARD MIGUEL'S EXAMINATION OF SUB-SA-haran Africa's economic development focuses on outside influences and interventions as the major economic forces affecting the region. Foreign aid, foreign direct investment, the co-lonial legacy, and so on: each plays a signifi-cant role in explaining the current status of the continent. Indeed, Miguel's focus may simply be a reflection of what has emerged over the past forty or fifty years as the prevailing view of the majority of Africans. According to this understanding, many Africans have been pas-sive victims, or beneficiaries, of outside initia-tives, lacking the money, tools, and resources to release themselves from their own economic shackles. I am not sure that this story was ever true. In any case, the current picture is very different. Moreover, while Miguel provides an analysis of formal development in sub-Saharan Africa, he ignores the crucial factor of informal economic growth. African entrepreneurs are discovering that the current technological environment enables them to remove those shackles for themselves. They need not rely on a donor agency or international trade agreement to hand them the key.

I have spent the past five years or so helping grassroots nonprofits in developing countries take advantage of the latest technological revolution—the mobile phone. With penetration rates in excess of 30 percent and handset sales among the highest in the world, sub-Saharan Africa is poised to gain from the introduction of what is commonly referred to as a "leapfrogging technology"—a technology that allows developing countries to bypass inferior methods and industries in favor of more advanced ones. Farmers are now able to access market information through their phones, and better information leads to higher income. Casual laborers are better able to advertise their services and take on more jobs because they spend less time waiting on street corners for work to come their way. Unemployed youth can receive news of job openings on their phones, alerting them when work becomes available. Web-enabled mobile phones can also provide health information and advice and remind people when to take their medicine. A citizen with a mobile phone has the information he or she needs to engage more actively in civil society by monitoring elections and helping keep governments accountable. Mobile telephony and Internet also make possible early warnings of wildlife threats, mitigating human-elephant conflict that endangers lives and livelihoods. The impact and wide-ranging uses of mobile technology in the developing world are nothing short of staggering.

The opportunities brought by the arrival of mobile technologies and services have not gone unnoticed, particularly by those at, or uncomfortably close to, the so-called bottom of the pyramid. There, too, mobile ownership is increasing, and shared phone and village phone schemes mean that those who are not yet able to afford a phone of their own still have access to the technology. A single village phone lady—an individual who purchases a mobile phone and charges neighbors for its use—may provide telecommunications services to hundreds of people in her area.

Mobile phones have become vital to the sub-Saharan way of life. According to the Center for Policy and Development, a Nigerian NGO, many Nigerians describe losing them as literally a matter of life or death for their businesses. More widely, the spread of mobile phones has created significant casual (or informal) employment opportunities. For example, a recent report by the Uganda Communications Commission found that that country's information communications technology sector, a majority of which is the mobile industry, officially employs roughly 6,000 people. The informal sector, which engages in support activities, represents over 350,000. The numbers are monumental. If we ignore this informal sector, a considerable amount of economic activity will be overlooked.

Anyone who has traveled to an African country in the past couple of years could not have failed to notice representatives or analogues of these 350,000 Ugandans: women selling airtime on the streets; children dodging cars at main junctions, selling chargers and phone covers; street vendors charging people's phones for a fee; and mobile phone repair shops squeezing one last drop of life from old phones. There is also a thriving second-hand market, with stalls selling all manner of new and recycled handsets. Entrepreneurs are even building their own traveling mobile services, strapping phones and spare batteries to the fronts of bikes and seeking out business.

In a much-cited 2005 study, an economist at the London Business School concluded that an extra ten mobile phones per hundred people in a "typical developing country" leads to a 0.59 percent increase in GDP per capita. The insatiable demand for mobile technology generates significant tax revenue for the government, but much of the growth can be found in the increasingly efficient informal sector, out of sight of governments and economists. At the bottom of the pyramid, where micro-loans of just a few dollars are a proven catalyst in helping people work their own way out of poverty, the diffusion of mobile technology has the clear potential to do the same.

As more and more people become connected, future studies of sub-Saharan Africa and its economic potential will find it increasingly difficult to ignore the influence of mobile technology and the spirit of African entrepreneurs who capitalize on it. There is little doubt that this spirit has always been there, but perhaps it is the emergence of mobile technology that has enabled it to thrive.

Olu Ajakaiye

IT IS IMPORTANT TO EXPLORE—AS EDWARD Miguel does—the factors responsible for the contemporary growth in sub-Saharan Africa, because we have been here before. In the first decade after independence, sub-Saharan countries recorded reasonable economic growth before a massive three-decades collapse. Understanding today's growth may help stem the risks of a new downturn in the second decade of the twenty-first century.

I also believe—along with Miguel—that Africa's recent gains in political freedom have played a role in the latest economic successes. A growing number of countries operate under democratic governance and enjoy the associated press freedoms, scrutiny of public office-holders, and rule of law. Punishment for those caught stealing at the ballot box may have played midwife to economic growth.

And China's contributions to new growth are not in doubt, as African countries now benefit directly or indirectly from high commodity prices; affordable Chinese imports; growing investment, especially in extractive industries; and, increasingly, development-augmenting aid packages for education and health. However, China's contributions pose certain challenges, namely, how to sustain growth when primary commodities continue to dominate Africa's output and income; the inevitable collapse of commodity prices as China engineers itself out of raw material–intensive production systems and into more knowledge-intensive ones; and the risk of so-called easy loans rekindling high debt in the future. How can African policy makers and researchers best avoid these hazards?

Miguel tucks into his discussion of China's role the important issue of access to U.S., EU, and Japanese markets. This is a crucial matter that requires greater consideration. With the related Economic Partnership Arrangements (EPAs) being actively promoted by the European Union, any discussion of Africa's economic future warrants a serious look at whether the European Union is friend or foe of today's African renaissance. The EPAs may present challenges to sustaining the current growth, challenges similar to those posed by the dominance of primary commodities in China-Africa trade. Another issue Miguel neglects is the need for African economies to build manufacturing capacity, and hence take advantage of access to world markets.

On the role of foreign aid, Miguel seems sympathetic to the view that Africa remains poor today despite hundreds of billions of dollars of foreign aid. Skepticism regarding the benefits of aid to countries plagued by corruption is fair, but one wonders if this is the whole story. This view assumes that there are no problems from the donor side. In fact, the donor community itself does not share this rather one-sided view, as evidenced by the spirit of the 2005 Paris Declaration on Aid Effectiveness.

On the issue of conflict costs and contagion, I, for the most part, agree that the impact on growth can be devastating. However, the proposition that if the economic growth of the last seven years continues for another decade or two African economies will be richer and more diversified and thus less at risk of falling into conflict has the feel of *mutatis mutandis*. Can we take for granted that diversification is in the offing? After all, the sub-Saharan growth process is driven mainly by primary commodities. What will ensure that growth is accompanied by equity, perceived or real? The root cause of conflicts in Africa is perceived or real economic and social inequality. We cannot assume away the challenges of economic diversification and equity. To sustain growth, policy makers must face them, and analysts must propose policies that can help achieve them.

The threat of climate change to the contemporary growth process is real and urgent. But Miguel gives the impression that, in spite of climate change, Africa will remain a primary commodities producer. This explains his almost exclusive attention to adaptation to drought through aid and research into drought-resistant crop varieties suited for the Sahel. With this kind of adaptation strategy, one wonders how African economies can become diversified, and thus less at risk of falling into conflict. I would have expected Miguel to also discuss the kinds of support that African countries would need in order to pursue clean development. African countries must have guaranteed access to green technologies so that, as their economies grow and diversify, they will not repeat the mistakes of advanced countries. Sub-Saharan Africa needs support for creating financial and other institutional structures that will enable it to develop in a climate-friendly way.

It is indeed too early to tell if Africa's time has come, but we must call for necessary action on the part of all stakeholders in African development to learn from recent success and give the continent its best chance to sustain those gains.

Rosamond Naylor

ALTHOUGH THE OVERALL ECONOMIC SITU-
ation in sub-Saharan Africa appears to have improved in recent years, any discussion about a
sustained turnaround for the region must consider the rural sector and the role of agricultural
development in improving the livelihood of
the poor. Even as better macroeconomic management and higher export commodity prices
have in recent years led to per capita income
growth in several countries, the poorest rural
populations—the landless or small landown-
ers who are net consumers of food—remain
desperately poor. According to World Bank
statistics, over half of sub-Saharan Africa's rural
population still lives in poverty, and the depth

of poverty is greater than in any other region of the world, with many surviving on roughly $0.60 per day.

Economic gains throughout the region have been far from equal, with income disparities growing both between and within countries. The gap in GDP per capita between the richest and poorest deciles of sub-Saharan African countries almost doubled from a factor of ten to eighteen between 1975 and 2005. Within two of the fastest-growing economies—oil-exporters Angola and Chad—the child mortality rates are 260 and 208 per 1,000, respectively, and the life expectancy at birth is 41 in the former, 44 in the latter. These grim statistics are comparable to those in two of the region's slowest-growing economies, Niger and Guinea-Bissau. Welfare measures in all of these countries could be improved with steady gains in rural development, particularly for small-scale farmers. But "steady" is not a word commonly used to describe the region. The economic growth process during the past three decades has been characterized by extreme volatility stemming from world commodity price fluctuations, conflict, weather shocks, and poor governance. Whether the region can sustain prolonged and widespread economic development remains to be seen.

There is no clearer evidence of the fragility of sub-Saharan Africa's economic progress than the current global food crisis. The United Nations Food and Agricultural Organization expects the annual cereal import bills of most countries in the region to rise by at least 75 percent this year (compared with 56 percent for low-income, food-importing countries outside the region), while import volumes are projected to decline. Increased demand for domestically grown crops, such as sorghum and millet, is pushing prices up for all commodities. Food riots have broken out in Burkina Faso, Côte d'Ivoire, Cameroon, Senegal, Mauritania, Ethiopia, Mozambique, Guinea, and Madagascar. In rural areas where staple crop yields are low, soil fertility is poor, and market access is weak, the silent swell of hunger continues to rise. Given that poor households already spend 60-80 percent of their incomes on staple foods, the price hikes translate directly into fewer and smaller meals per day. World Bank president Robert Zoellick projects that the ongoing food crisis is likely to eliminate virtually all gains in poverty and hunger reduction achieved since the Millennium Development Goals were established in 2000.

The global food crisis highlights three points crucial to sub-Saharan Africa's development process. First, international and domestic investments in agricultural productivity for staple crops in the region have been woefully inadequate during the past few decades. In 2000 sub-Saharan Africa received only 6.3 percent of global public expenditures and 0.2 percent of global private expenditures on agricultural research and development. As a result, even in rain-fed areas, the region has not experienced anything close to the agricultural productivity success experienced in the rest of the developing world for the last 30 years. Moreover, high population growth is creating an even greater need for yield increases. Large "exploitable yield gaps" (the difference between yields in farmers' fields and yields at crop research stations) exist for most staple crops, but fertilizer and water are lacking, as are critical institutional structures like well-functioning credit, seed, fertilizer, and product markets, and methods for managing risks, particularly for smallholders.

Second, the current high-price environment for essential food crops provides a powerful incentive for agricultural investments in sub-Saharan Africa. But such investments will likely come from both the public and private sectors, not smallholder farmers. The latter simply do not have the resources to respond to price incentives through agricultural investments, especially since their (net) food expenditures are increasing. A 2000 Michigan State University study of the Zambian maize sector found that 2 percent of all farmers accounted for one half of total maize sales in the country. The other half came from 23 percent of the farmers, leaving the remaining 75 percent of maize producers consuming virtually all of their output at home. The challenge in the near term will be to design and execute investment strategies that actually reach the poor, rather than tilting the balance further toward larger farmers. Improving livelihoods of the poorest populations will require political will and a focus on equity, agricultural productivity, and nutritional outcomes.

Finally, with only 4 percent of the region's agricultural land under irrigation, the rural economy is likely to suffer significantly from climate change over the next twenty-five years and beyond, unless substantial efforts are made to help farmers adapt. Higher temperatures, declining soil moisture, and variable rainfall will make farming more difficult in most areas. Miguel discusses this danger with reference to the results of one climate model applied to the Sahel. Researchers at Stanford University conducted a more thorough analysis of climate risks for almost two dozen crops in the region. It shows that by 2030 southern African maize production is likely to fall by 30 percent, while several other African crops (millet, cowpea, wheat) will likely fall by 10-15 percent. The projections mark early warnings of change. The models indicate that, by mid-century, temperature will already be out of bounds from what is experienced today: the coldest years in the future will still be warmer than the hottest years in the past century.

What this dramatic shift in climate means for agriculture, migration, and economic growth in sub-Saharan Africa depends to a great extent on future investments in rural development. Strategies for crop breeding programs, small-scale irrigation, and risk-management schemes for the poor need to be high on the political agendas of sub-Saharan countries and the international community. As the present food crisis sadly suggests, Africa will reach a sustained turnaround only when its people can afford to eat.

David N. Weil

I SHARE EDWARD MIGUEL'S CAUTIOUS optimism: the new millennium has started out well for Africa. Democracy is making steady progress, with genuinely contested elections more common and the press increasingly free. Per-capita GDP is growing at an average rate of 3 percent per year—not East Asian–miracle levels, but quite respectable for any developing country, and a sea change from the previous several decades in Africa. Foreign investment is rising, inflation has dropped in most countries, debt has fallen, and foreign exchange reserves have risen. High commodity prices have been a big driver of African growth, but there is evidence that the current boom is more broadly based. The explosive growth in cell phone use (from 7.5 million users in 1999 to 100 million today), which is making markets more efficient and alleviating Africa's curse of bad transportation networks, shows how technology and entrepreneurial innovation can radically change the economic environment. Finally, rapid economic growth in the rest of the developing world, particularly China and India, can only be to Africa's advantage, and not only by raising commodity prices. As other countries get rich, there will be more demand for expensive sport shoes, and fewer people in the world poor enough to stitch them—and so the jobs (and millions like them) may migrate to Africa.

I also agree with Miguel that political developments on the continent will be critical to determining whether current growth in Africa will hold: war, instability, or a return to inept governance can easily stall gains for several decades.

But Miguel is silent on an important issue affecting Africa's economic future: population growth. Start with the numbers: While world population as a whole has grown by a factor of 2.6 since 1950, in Africa it grew by a factor of 4.3. In 2005, 753 million people lived in sub-Saharan Africa. The United Nations forecasts that between 2005 and 2050, the population of Africa will increase by a factor of 2.3. In Kenya, the country on which Miguel focuses, population grew from 13.5 million in 1975 to 35.6 million today, and is forecast to reach 84.8 million by 2050.

The primary reason for Africa's rapid population growth is what demographers call a "stalled demographic transition." In the decades following World War II, mortality rates on the continent declined sharply as medical and public health technologies from rich countries rapidly diffused. Historically, and in other parts of the world, such mortality declines are usually followed, within a generation or two, by similar declines in fertility to a level commensurate with relatively stable population. But in Africa the decline in fertility has been very slow, with the number of children per woman falling from 6.7 to 5.3 between 1950 and 2005. By contrast, fertility in Southeast Asia fell from 6.0 children per woman to 2.5 over the same period.

The reasons declining fertility has trailed so much behind declining mortality in Africa are not fully understood. Cultural factors—including the low status of women—are clearly at work. The fact that Africa experienced a decline in mortality at a level of income much lower than the rest of the world is probably part of the story, too. Furthermore, mortality levels have not fallen as low as elsewhere in the developing world. Family planning's departure from the international development agenda while fertility in Africa was still high may also have played a small role.

Rapid population growth has produced sufficient "demographic momentum" that even if the current fertility rate declines precipitously, population will continue to grow quickly for several generations. Indeed, the UN forecast assumes a relatively steep fall in fertility, from its current level of 5.3 children per woman to 2.5 by 2050. If fertility does not fall so quickly, population growth will be even higher.

Thus, failing some catastrophe of unprecedented proportions, Africa is going to experience a huge increase in population over the next several decades. How will that population growth affect economic development? Discussions of this issue tend to fall into one of two camps: apocalyptic and dismissive. The middle-ground view—that rapid population growth makes development more difficult but not impossible—is surprisingly unpopular.

The most obvious dimension along which population growth will matter is food. Africa already skates along the edge of food shortage. In 2005, 29 percent of children under five were underweight. Africa is currently a small net importer of grain, but with food prices on international markets scaling new heights, food grown outside the continent is unlikely to fill many bellies.

All this would be a recipe for disaster if Africa could not grow enough food for itself, but in fact it can. For a variety of reasons, African agriculture is extraordinarily unproductive in terms of food output relative to land and labor resources used. The yield of maize—one of the region's primary food crops—per acre planted has been unchanged in sub-Saharan Africa since 1975; over the same period yields more than doubled in every other region of the developing world. Per-acre grain yields in Kenya, which is among Africa's most productive countries, are two-thirds the level of India, and slightly more than half those in Mexico.

Some of Africa's low agricultural productivity is due to climate and geography, but a good deal is man-made. Sub-Saharan Africa, excluding South Africa, accounts for only 1 percent of world fertilizer use. Only 20 percent of the area sown in maize uses modern varieties, compared to more than 50 percent in South Asia and Latin America. Irrigation is rare (4 percent of farm land, as opposed to 37 percent in Asia), even where it is technically feasible.

Why does a region capable of providing for itself maintain such poor agricultural practice? The problem lies in the economic and institutional arrangements that determine farmers' options. African governments spent much of the post-independence period creating institutions—such as marketing boards and price controls—that disadvantaged farmers for the benefit of city dwellers. Fertilizer use stagnated in the 1980s as governments removed subsidies in the face of massive budget deficits. The private sector has not filled the vacuum left by the dismemberment of parastatal—state-owned and partially state-owned—companies; facilities to advance credit to farmers to pay for fertilizer and seeds, and to provide insurance against bad weather that would make borrowing possible, have not developed. Because of its unique ecology, Africa has been unable to make much use of agricultural technology that raised productivity in most of the rest of the world, and its governments—weak and with other priorities—have not built the research infrastructure necessary to tailor crops to local conditions.

In addition, pressure to feed a growing population has led to shortening of fallow periods and overgrazing, which have degraded soil quality. The area of land under cultivation has increased by 80 percent since 1960, with much of the newly cultivated land of marginal quality. Three quarters of farmland in sub-Saharan Africa has suffered significant depletion of soil nutrients.

The good news is that to the extent that low agricultural productivity is a man-made problem, it can readily be fixed. The Millennium Villages project has shown that providing fertilizer and improved seeds to African farmers can have an enormous positive effect on agricultural productivity. The yield gap between typical farms and demonstration plots using best available techniques is a factor of three. The Alliance for a Green Revolution in Africa is working to develop improved seeds, educate farmers, and improve the distribution systems for agricultural inputs.

A second dimension along which population will matter is urbanization. Africa is the least urban continent, but also the most rapidly urbanizing, with urban populations growing at 5 percent per year. Seventy percent of Africa's urban population lives in slums, with most living in improvised dwellings of scrap lumber, corrugated metal, and plastic sheeting. Terrible crowding along with a lack of sanitation and clean water make urban slums hotbeds for disease. And yet for the majority of residents, this lifestyle represents an improvement over the rural poverty they fled.

Once again, rapid urbanization can be a recipe for disaster, but it does not have to be. Largely a problem in governance and institutions, improving living standards in African cities requires spending on infrastructure and the political will to grant slum dwellers ownership of the land on which they currently squat. Even more significantly, urban poverty will only be ameliorated by the creation of an institutional environment in which private businesses can thrive. The vast number of informal enterprises present in the typical urban slum is testament to the entrepreneurial energy of the residents as well as the legal environment that makes opening a formal business impossible. But only formal businesses, which have better access to credit and can use the legal system to enforce contracts, are going to grow large enough to create jobs. The world is awash in capital that would readily flow to Africa to take advantage of abundant cheap labor, if there were good governance. Low corruption and rule of law are crucial.

Rapid population growth will make good governance harder to achieve. It puts great strain on government finance, as schools and infrastructure must be provided for ever more people. More directly, higher population exacerbates land scarcity, which is a potentially explosive issue. Land shortages are thought to have been one of the preconditions for the horrific ethnic violence that exploded in Rwanda and Burundi in the mid-1990s, and the recent post-election violence in Kenya was driven by politicians exploiting a widespread sense of injustice regarding the distribution of land. Urbanization may also hinder the establishment of good governance. Urban slums, lawless to begin with, and well stocked with young men who have little to lose, are potential flashpoints for political violence, as was the case in Kenya.

Neither food shortage nor urbanization need spell disaster for Africa, but they raise the stakes for the performance of African governments. If governments tack back toward old dysfunctional ways, they are unlikely to head off catastrophe. Political violence will scare away the foreign donors who are investing in the future of African agriculture, as well as the foreign trade and capital required to provide jobs for urban slum dwellers.

Jeremy M. Weinstein

WHILE THE SMALL (BUT NOTICEABLE) UPTICK in Africa's recent economic growth is not in dispute, its causes are not entirely clear. Like Miguel, I would like to believe that democratic reforms deserve some credit for this unexpected turn of events. Most African countries today hold regular elections, and political leaders in Africa are significantly more likely to leave power voluntarily than through a coup, violent overthrow, or assassination.

Yet it has been frustratingly difficult for social scientists to find robust evidence of democracy's economic dividends. Analyses of global trends often yield contradictory findings. And there is disagreement both about the data and how it should be analyzed. One recent study, for example, suggests that the poverty-reducing potential of democracies has been overstated simply because the datasets researchers use tend to lack information about the most successful autocratic regimes. Causation is an even harder nut to crack, as there are compelling arguments suggesting that economic growth spurs democracy and not vice versa. Some recent evidence from Africa points to increased spending on primary schools and reductions in infant mortality following the democratic transitions of the early 1990s, but as the graphs in Miguel's essay make clear, recent increases in GDP per capita have come nearly ten years after the wave of political reforms began.

The absence of convincing evidence linking democracy to economic growth is surprising. One would expect societies with democratic processes to better police the behavior of politicians and bureaucrats, thereby ensuring more responsible policy choices. Societies in which a greater share of the population plays a role in selecting leaders should also have policies that are more broadly beneficial. The story is plausible, and I am still prepared to believe it, but there is reason to suspect that Africa's recent economic good fortune has little to do with democratization.

We might ask ourselves whether Africa's new democracies are, in fact, democracies at all. Many observers of African politics were too hasty in crediting countries with having transitioned to democracy, simply because those countries held elections. In 2002 Thomas Carothers famously penned an epitaph for the "transition paradigm," critiquing the long-dominant notions in aid circles that any move away from dictatorship is a move toward democracy, that transitions unfold in a sequence that inevitably results in democracy, and that elections are determinative in bringing about a democratic political order.

Reality looks much messier. The majority of countries that initiated elections in the early 1990s are in what Carothers terms the "gray zone," as "pseudo-democracies" or "hybrid regimes." African governments have often done the bare minimum to appease outside donors pressing for political change—holding elections, permitting opposition parties to contest—while avoiding reforms that might truly level the playing field. Many African democracies, in practice, are controlled by a single political coalition that blurs the line between state and ruling party and sees government assets as tools for enhancing its political domination. Recent booms in commodity prices and the growing importance of unconditional Chinese aid and investment further undermine the incentives that might induce leaders to permit real political competition. And a closer look at Africa's economic success stories—Equatorial Guinea, Chad, Angola, and Sudan (among oil producers); Mozambique, Rwanda,

Botswana, and Uganda (among diversified economies)—should give us additional pause. In the last decade, not one has experienced a peaceful transfer of power between political parties. For many political scientists, alternation between governing parties is the sine qua non of democracy.

A less familiar, but equally important, reason for questioning the link between Africa's recent progress and democratization is the fact that democratic politics can have its own pathologies, pathologies that are especially apparent in weak democracies. In highly diverse societies—and Africa is composed of the most ethnically heterogeneous countries in the world—democratic competition is often reduced to an ethnic head count. Parties are mobilized along ethnic lines, as groups compete with one another for control of the state budget. As we saw so tragically in Kenya in December, politicians can successfully exploit simmering ethnic tension to consolidate support, even when their performance in office would hardly merit re-election.

Moreover, democratic transitions are, by definition, unstable—a fact that might account for the stubborn persistence of civil war in Africa, even during a decade of substantial political liberalization. War scares off foreign investors, distorts the economy, and undermines incentives for good public policy and domestic investment. Democracy can only bridge deep social and economic divides when people have faith that government institutions serve interests beyond those of the group that temporarily inhabits office.

I do not raise the question of whether we can truly credit Africa's recent economic success to its democratic progress in order to rebut the general importance of liberal institutions for growth. But, given the state of African democracy, it seems more likely that rising commodity prices and increasing Chinese aid and investment are doing much of the work. This may represent good news in the short term (and the World Bank has trumpeted it as such), but the danger is that Africa's development miracle will be short-lived. Only a firmer institutional foundation can sustain it.

Democracy can create the conditions for development, but only when its protectors (and strongest advocates)—the voters—are in a position to observe how politicians behave and choose to replace them if they fail to deliver. The good news is that it is becoming increasingly difficult for ruling parties to hang on to power unfairly. Mechanisms that generate transparency—such as access to media, cell phones, and the Internet—are making a huge difference. Exit polling sent strong signals to the opposition in Kenya that they had actually won the election. The public posting of precinct results in Zimbabwe—a key concession won by the Movement for Democratic Change in pre-election negotiations—provided the basis for its candidate's claim to have defeated Robert Mugabe.

More broadly, efforts to shed light on the behavior of governments and inform voters are yielding real benefits. Uganda has been an important laboratory. Greater transparency in public expenditures has led to a dramatic increase in the share of government revenue allocated to education that has actually made its way to the schools. Community-based monitoring of government health centers has inspired higher quality care. And efforts to inform voters about what their Members of Parliament do are radically changing politicians' incentives to be active in the legislature.

Decades of dictatorship coincided with a period of economic decline and stagnation in Africa. That the Amins, Mobutus, and Bokassas now inhabit only the pages of history books may be bearing some fruit, as Miguel argues. But the extent of institutional reform should not be overstated; more work remains to be done. As greater transparency and more credible institutions are established, perhaps the economic dividends of democracy will no longer be so difficult to uncover.

Smita Singh

EDWARD MIGUEL SUGGESTS SEVERAL REASONS to be hopeful about Africa's economic prospects and a few causes for concern. One in each category, democratic governance and climate change, deserve further elaboration.

First, democratic governance. Miguel rightly lauds the almost continent-wide movement toward greater democratization. Despite Kenya's recent electoral setbacks, Miguel is right that "opposition parties are ubiquitous and open debate the norm in a growing number of African countries." But reaping the economic fruits of democratization will require more than multi-party elections. Elections in and of themselves need not force leaders to be responsive to the public good; electoral competition can drive political parties into patronage instead. Scholars studying African politics are divided on whether democracy is beneficial to African economies.

Miguel argues that, on balance, democracy has been good for Africa. But if elections are not sufficient to consolidate the political, social, and economic gains of democracy, then what is? What more does Africa need? The answer lies in transparency and accountability mechanisms that provide checks and balances, particularly in regard to public spending.

Public spending often determines whether democracy delivers for the average citizen. Are roads built so she can get her crop to market? Are textbooks available in the school for her children? Is the local health clinic staffed? It's not just a matter of attention-grabbing corruption and malfeasance, but more importantly of creating incentives for the efficient allocation and use of public resources.

Scrutiny of budget allocations, tracking of actual expenditures, and the monitoring and evaluation of service delivery are vital watchdog functions for independent civil society organizations, the media, parliaments, and executive audit agencies. Consider the benefits. In one case, comparative cost surveys carried out by a policy research organization across municipalities in an Indian state highlighted the differential costs of public services, spurring bureaucrats in high-cost towns to lower their procurement costs. Successful fulfillment of these important watchdog functions requires transparency.

Of course, it is easier to set up elections than effective public accountability mechanisms. Indeed, donors have traditionally spent much more money and time focusing on the development of elections than other techniques for public scrutiny. Our collective knowledge of how to build a system of checks and balances, which is necessarily context-dependent, lags far behind our knowledge in other areas. Research devoted to improving efficiency and reducing corruption in public works projects, for example, is helping us get beyond simple notions of community monitoring as the best or only means of achieving public accountability. But more investment in learning which accountability mechanisms work best under which circumstances would be well worth making.

We should not pretend that transparency and accountability are not critical to the continent's economic future. Whether Africa's current commodity boom is harnessed for long-term development or simply leads to a repeat of the dismal economic performance that followed the commodity boom of the mid-1970s will depend in part on the checks and balances Africans establish to constrain the management of revenues and expenditures.

Second, climate change. In what is surely one of the most troubling ironies of our time, the people who have contributed the least to climate change will suffer the most from its effects. Although rich countries have caused the problem with decades of greenhouse-gas emissions, developing countries are the most vulnerable. Many African countries will be hit especially hard, as Miguel points out.

According to the April 2007 report of the Intergovernmental Panel on Climate Change (IPCC), the poor will bear the brunt of climate risks. The IPCC report concludes that "even the most stringent mitigation efforts cannot avoid further impacts of climate change in the next few decades, which makes adaptation essential." Miguel suggests tailored drought insurance mechanisms and agricultural research as two necessary adaptation measures.

I couldn't agree more, but there is a larger point to be made: one of the key determinants of a society's capacity to adapt to climate change is access to resources. For example, smallholder farmers lack the resources to invest in basic adaptation measures—such as improved irrigation and fertilization—that would better insulate them from shifts in weather patterns. Therefore, equitable economic growth is urgently needed to arm the world's poorest people with the resources to adapt to climate change.

Researchers are now recognizing that equitable development and adaptive capacity for coping with climate change actually rely on a common set of conditions. Unless this complementarity between equitable development and adaptive capacity is widely understood, there is a risk that additional financing for climate adaptation could displace investments in economic growth and poverty reduction. This would be a huge mistake, since the key is to build the capacity of societies to adapt to and mitigate climate change over the longer term.

If you care about poverty in Africa, you can't ignore the impact of climate change, and if you care about climate change, you can't ignore economic development in Africa. It is therefore imperative to tackle both of these challenges simultaneously. However, this is not happening. Poorly thought-out biofuels policies pushed by some environmentalists have helped spark a world food crisis, while not doing much, it turns out, to mitigate climate change once land-use changes are taken into account. A similar harmful potential exists for other climate policy proposals that fail to account for secondary effects. Unless we consider the development consequences of our policy solutions, Africa's poor will face not only the worst effects of climate change, but the worst effects of the policy interventions, too.

Paul Collier

EDWARD MIGUEL IS AN ASTUTE OBSERVER of Africa. I particularly admire his combination of insights from fieldwork with an analysis of the big picture, but let me try to offer something more useful than praise.

I wrote *The Bottom Billion* in 2005. Given the lags in economic data, it was only possible to track African economic performance until around 2002, so the millennium was a natural place to draw the line. As Miguel's chart of income shows, the early cutoff misses something important: since the turn of the millennium, there has been a boom at the bottom. Obviously, the key question is whether this marks a real break with past trends or a blip.

I rather doubt that the wave of democratization has driven the economic turnaround. I would dearly like to believe that it has, but Africa's democracies basically amount to elections without checks and balances. The inevitable happens: incumbents use the opportunity of freedom from checks and balances to manipulate elections. Miguel writes of Kenya, but a far more dramatic episode has rapidly superseded the Kenyan election. As I write, President Robert Mugabe has turned Zimbabwean democracy into farce. Furthermore, there can be little doubt that the Zimbabwean economy has suffered because of the election. In order to win, Mugabe has uprooted the rule of law, and this has had severe economic consequences. My forthcoming book, *State of War*, sets out why I think democracy has gone wrong in the bottom billion and what would be needed to put it on track.

If democracy is not responsible for the economic about-face, what is? Miguel considers commodity booms an important factor. Indeed, in the short term a country exporting commodities in high demand cannot help but grow. The issue is whether the revenues can be harnessed for something sustainable. Most African governments failed to do so during the last commodity booms of the 1970s. The vital task for Africa now is avoiding a repetition of history.

But the growth we are seeing today is not just a result of commodity booms. I don't think that is the key to Kenya's pre-election economic success. There is a process at work that does not depend on democracy and is so simple that analysts generally miss it: learning from mistakes. Since 1970 African societies have accumulated a huge stock of experience in how not to manage an economy. For example, from the mid-1970s until the mid-1980s Tanzania adopted regulatory policies that proved to be ruinous. The knowledge they gained through failure is valuable. Tanzania is now one of the best-managed of all Africa's economies. The European society with the best record of containing inflation over the past sixty years is Germany. It has the best record because it used to have the worst: the experience of hyperinflation immunized Germans from macroeconomic folly.

Learning from failure is an unglamorous and sometimes unpopular explanation for Africa's improvement. But if it is right it has one hugely important and attractive implication: the improvement is robust. I am hopeful that the present commodity booms will be better handled than those of the 1970s, primarily because many Africans are fully aware of past mistakes and are determined not to repeat them.

Rachel Glennerster

THE SOFT WINDS OF THE INDIAN OCEAN
and the view from the cliffs overlooking Maputo would be enough to make anyone fall in
love with southern Africa. But my trip to Mozambique in 2001 (and my subsequent work
there) did much more than that—it made me
an optimist about Africa. Peace, democracy,
market-friendly policies, and investment and
trade with South Africa had already led to nine
years of impressive growth. The prospects for
the future looked even better—much of Mozambique's official debt was about to be can-
celled, foreign investment was flooding in, and
export projections were spectacular. As of writ-
ing, Mozambique has enjoyed fifteen years of

8 percent-per-year growth and a sharp reduction in poverty. Even more encouragingly, the list of African countries experiencing sustained growth is lengthening.

Edward Miguel discusses some of the potential reasons for the upswing in growth and warns that conflict, which continues to devastate important regions of the continent, could all too easily shatter these hopeful trends. Making generalizations about a continent as large and diverse as Africa is perilous, but some trends do shine through. Miguel focuses on improvements in democracy and terms of trade, and points to the influence of Chinese investment. He is somewhat dismissive of the role aid has played and calls for reductions in agricultural subsidies to further improve African terms of trade. I, too, will focus on China, trade, and aid, issues on which I have a somewhat different take.

Chinese investment in Africa has been celebrated for reducing the influence of old colonial powers, and feared as the start of a new debt spiral. But China's increasing economic presence in Africa may be more notable for its suddenness than its size. And sudden changes in flows of investment are often not sustained for long periods. Before we get carried away about Chinese investment it is worth noting that the entire stock of Chinese foreign direct investment (FDI) in Africa in 2005 was just one-tenth of the flow of new FDI from the United Kingdom into Africa the previous year.

Potentially more important than the import of capital has been the import of cheap manufactured goods from China, which has enabled Africans to afford products they would not otherwise have been able to enjoy. Cheap Chinese bicycles are everywhere in Busia, the Kenyan town Miguel describes. They help transport agricultural produce to market and are the basis of a thriving taxi trade whereby customers sit sidesaddle on the back. In Sierra Leone, where the radio is a key source of information about politics, cheap Chinese radios are helping inform and connect a highly dispersed population.

The commodity price boom—whether generated by China or not—has indeed helped sub-Saharan Africa, which has experienced a 50 percent increase in total trade since 2000. But it would be wrong to conclude that further price rises of agricultural products, which would likely follow a cut in rich country agricultural subsidies, would necessarily benefit Africa. While sub-Saharan Africa is a net exporter of cotton, it is a net importer of basic foodstuffs such as maize and wheat, which means that, on average, it gains from rich country subsidies on these products.

Miguel concludes that aid can explain neither Africa's growth, which picked up in the mid-'90s and accelerated around 2000, nor its improved democratic or educational institutions, because aid first fell and then rose during the 1990s and 2000s. But this claim misses the dramatic change in aid-distribution philosophy that took root during that period. During the Cold War, aid was often used to support "our" despots no matter how bad their policies. The dramatic fall in aid in the 1990s in part reflects cutting off those dictators. Donors became more selective about whom they would support and tied aid in countries like Kenya to moves toward democracy and control of corruption. Is it not at least possible that this "housecleaning" supported or even triggered some of the moves to democracy observed shortly afterwards? Democractic advancements in turn have helped deliver the improvements in access to education Miguel points to, as politicians discover that voters like the idea of abolishing fees for primary health care and education.

It is easy to point to the ongoing corruption scandals and vote rigging in Kenya as evidence of the failure of this policy, but would we (or, more importantly, would Kenyans) prefer to return to the days when criticism of government or mention of AIDS were barred in the press, as was the case when I first visited Kenya in 1986? Let us not fall into the trap of equating lack of complete success with failure, as is common in the discussions of aid.

How big a factor in Africa's success was the release of aid from the political constraints of the Cold War? It is impossible to say, because it coincided with a recognition within African governments that planning was not going to deliver development, and that market-price signals and economic stability were powerful tools in generating growth. In Mozambique in 2001, I watched the minister of finance berate her colleagues for even daring to think of risking long-run economic stability for short-run political gain. More than the new heavily export-oriented investment projects opening in Maputo, it was this that made me optimistic. Is there room to improve the way aid supports the governments of countries like Mozambique? Absolutely, and that is what many economists—Miguel included—now do through careful impact evaluations. But was the hand of the finance minister strengthened by the philosophical and financial support of the donors, responsible for 40 percent of the budget? You bet.

III

*Real
Progress*

THIS BOOK WAS COMPLETED IN MARCH 2008, and highlights Africa's encouraging economic and political trends. Those encouraging trends have continued, while some new challenges have come into sharper focus. African societies (like all societies) are complicated systems, and many gains are fragile. But the progress I described is real and can no longer be ignored.

Kenya again provides a useful starting point in thinking about sub-Saharan Africa as a whole. The contested December 2007 national election that erupted in violence eventually led to a power-sharing arrangement between President Mwai Kibaki and his main election challenger, the new Prime Minister Raila Odinga. The unprecedented deal was brokered through extensive international arm-twisting administered by former UN Secretary General Kofi Annan. Kenyans of all political persuasions have since been wondering whether, and for how long, the deal will hold. The good news is that—at least so far—power-sharing has ended the violence and led to a number of welcome changes.

The most immediate moves were the constitutional reforms needed to implement the power-sharing deal, including the creation of the prime ministership. But providing Odinga's Orange Democratic Movement with real political power has had other payoffs, leading to more profound democratic transformation. Kenyan courts have recently recognized, and agreed to remunerate, citizens tortured by President Moi's security services during the 1980s and 1990s, generating hope that condemning past crimes will help curtail future human rights violations. Former anti-corruption czar John Githongo, who went into exile in 2005 after uncovering dirty insider dealings in Kibaki's regime, felt safe enough to return to Kenya in August 2008. His formidable voice will rejoin local calls for improved governance.

These changes do not, of course, mean that all is well in Kenyan politics. Both camps are maneuvering to enact their preferred reforms and take credit for economic growth. But the shift from dueling ethnic militias to debating parliamentarians is a huge step forward.

The Kenyan economy took a major hit during the 2008 political crisis. Firms throughout the country were shut down for months as the power struggle played itself out on the streets, and trade suffered as transport links were cut. But after the negotiations succeeded, there was a stunningly swift return to normal economic life for most Kenyans. Shops and factories reopened. Tourists and foreign investors returned. Cut-flower farmers could once again fly their precious cargo to European markets. And after dropping by nearly 25 percent at the height of the political crisis, the Nairobi Stock Exchange rebounded above its previous high by late April 2008. Despite the turmoil, Kenya's economic growth still looks to be positive in 2008.

Kenya's institutions and economy both proved resilient following the stolen elections. But the power-sharing deal could still unravel, particularly if President Kibaki backtracks on his promises to Odinga (as he did in 2003). There will be new national elections in 2012 at the latest, with their built-in risk of ethnic violence and instability. Elections can breed instability in young democracies, and not only in Kenya. In some recent research, my colleagues and I show that many Africans' ethnic identities harden substantially in the months preceding and following competitive democratic elections, most likely because politicians find it advantageous to play the ethnic card.

Can Kenyan democracy survive another close election?

The rest of Africa had an even better 2008 than Kenya, economically speaking. Preliminary estimates from early 2008 indicate that African economic growth rates have remained high, extending the upswing I described in my essay. High export prices and inflows of foreign capital, including from Asia, continue to play a leading role.

But several major risks, both economic and political, remain, and new ones have surfaced. The first concern is a South African meltdown. Because of its industrial might, South Africa is playing a giant role in Africa's economic recovery: it has been a major force for investment and trade since the fall of apartheid, and the leading migration destination for its neighbors. Its democratic opening has inspired the world. So much is riding on its steady (if slow) economic growth that political instability in the aftermath of the 2009 national polls could have massive spillover consequences for Africa's economic future.

The rise of Jacob Zuma—recently investigated for both corruption and rape—to leadership within the ruling African National Congress has raised fears about South Africa's future political leadership. Certainly, no leader of South Africa can ever again have Nelson Mandela's national and international stature, and it wouldn't be fair to set the bar that high. But will the next generation of South African leaders have the wisdom and patience not to kill the goose that laid the golden egg—South Africa's prosperous economy? For all of his flaws, especially his bizarre denial of the role of HIV in the AIDS crisis, Thabo Mbeki has at least restrained the more populist economic proposals of some of his supporters, presiding over stable macroeconomic and fiscal policies that have allowed for steady economic expansion.

A second risk is that the unprecedented run up in global commodity prices might end, threatening the livelihoods of millions of Africans who work in commodity-export industries and drying up government revenue. This year (2008) has seen the first sustained drop in a range of commodity prices in at least six years, including a 50 percent drop (as I write) in oil prices from their peak. African countries, including Nigeria, Gabon, Sudan, Chad, and Angola, among others, are deeply reliant on petroleum exports. When oil prices fall, public education, health, and agriculture programs are threatened along with the payment of police and army salaries. A parallel logic applies to countries whose populations—and state coffers—rely on coffee or copper exports. The spreading world financial crisis that exploded in September 2008 threatens to push the global economy into recession, and demand for Africa's commodity exports down with it. A few years from now, 2008 might represent another turning point in Africa's economic development trajectory, this time negative.

Eroding livelihoods and weakening state repressive law-and-order capacity are a volatile mix in poor countries. A sharp drop in export commodity prices, like other economic shocks, could translate into greater risk of political instability and even civil war in many African countries. This is arguably a moment when new foreign aid mechanisms, like the rapid conflict prevention support proposal I described in my opening essay, are called for. Acting fast may be critical to stopping the spiral into political instability and violence, but unfortunately such initiatives have yet to appear (to my knowledge) on the horizon among development policymakers. In fact, in the October 2008 Vice Presidential debate, Senator Joseph Biden explicitly singled out foreign aid as an area where the U.S. government should make sharp cuts due to the economic crisis, likely leaving little scope for creative new programs like those I propose.

Beyond responding to the challenges posed by the (seeming) end of high commodity export prices, foreign donors' ideal role in the next chapter of African development remains highly contested. One possible role is a greater emphasis on promoting institutional reform, including democratic transformation. The recent Kenyan power-sharing deal is an example of how foreign-aid donors can play such a constructive role. Both the recent political settlement and Kenya's earlier 1992 opening to multi-party competition were facilitated by serious international pressure, especially from the European Union and the United States.

However, few of Kenya's African neighbors have received the same level of donor engagement. Foreign aid has rarely been employed as a force for constructive political reform in Africa in the recent past, with Western support for human rights and democracy typically more rhetoric than reality. In the 1990s large foreign-aid donors (including the World Bank) lavished financial support on Uganda, a one-party regime that meddled militarily in its neighbors' affairs, looting piles of diamonds from war-torn Congo along the way. The United States and France today are far more interested in securing a stable supply of petroleum from Nigeria, Gabon, and Angola than in investigating credible claims about election rigging. The rise of Asian economic influence in Africa may further weaken international pressures for political reform. New evidence suggests that growing economic interactions with China—in particular through the commodities trade—could lead to less democratic institutions, presumably by insulating African political leaders from reform pressures.

What is the way forward, then? A critical issue for African countries trying to sustain their current economic booms is to learn from their own pasts and avoid the unsuccessful policies adopted during—and in the immediate aftermath—of the 1970s commodity boom, the closest historical analogue. The question for those African leaders interested in promoting robust economic growth is how to choose the right policies.

Part of the answer, I believe, lies in rigorous impact evaluations. Such evaluations are a promising tool for African policymakers and donors alike. Following a methodology similar to our counterparts in the medical sciences, economists have in recent years started taking the lessons of randomized trials to heart. One place to witness this new approach in action is in Kenya's Busia district. The economists working in Busia—led by Harvard economist Michael Kremer, and including myself—are at the forefront of a movement to better understand what works in development. In collaboration with NGOs, academic researchers working in Busia used randomized program evaluations to show that providing anti-parasitic drugs for intestinal worms—a major scourge affecting over 90 percent of Busia's children—can boost primary school attendance. Comparing deworming to other common interventions shows that it is arguably the most cost-effective way to achieve attendance gains in rural Africa. Just as medical researchers are confident that new therapies are responsible for health improvements among their treatment group, we can be sure that anti-parasitic drugs are responsible for higher school attendance.

While success stories such as deworming draw most attention, randomized evaluations do not always produce positive results about program impacts. But knowing about failures is equally useful; it allows policymakers to shift funding from the projects that do not work toward those that do. This is at the heart of the learning agenda that many economists, including myself, believe is the key to Africa's economic future. Emerging democracies are particularly good learning environments. There, impact evaluations can be carried out, their fruits widely distributed by an unfettered media, and governments held accountable for applying their lessons to policy.

With impact-evaluation results in hand, policymakers in poor countries will increasingly be able to rely on hard evidence when deciding how to use their scarce resources. We now know the benefits of anti-parasitic drugs in improving school attendance in Busia, and as a result the Kenyan national government has included mass school-based deworming in its official school health plan for the country. Word has spread, and other African countries have expanded their own school deworming plans. In Ghana, over four million children received anti-parasitic drugs at school in 2007.

Learning about deworming is a small step forward on its own. But it will be through many such small lessons—in areas as diverse as health, education, agriculture, governance, and foreign aid, and through both rigorous impact evaluations and other forms of learning about successful public policies—that African countries might learn to sustain and possibly augment their recent economic growth, even after the inevitable fall in global commodity prices.

Beyond improving the efficiency of government resource allocation, rigorous impact evaluations could have political benefits. In nations with weaker governance, rigorous program evaluations can themselves serve as a form of political accountability, empowering decent government officials to push for reform. The simple fact that someone is keeping track of where public resources are going, and who's benefiting from them, may constrain the most egregious forms of corruption and waste. In polities with deep social divisions, objective evidence about which programs are most effective can help build consensus around a set of public policies, while simultaneously battling despair about how "nothing works." Identifying and delivering effective anti-poverty programs could provide a reformist government with the enhanced political legitimacy needed to pursue ambitious institutional changes.

Kenya's post-election crisis makes clear the limits of its democratic reforms and its lingering social divisions. But it has also highlighted the remarkable resilience and creativity of Kenyans themselves: they looked national disintegration in the face and were forced to re-imagine the future of their society. If other African countries follow Kenyans in fighting for their democracy and in learning about the best economic policies for their own societies, sub-Saharan Africa's long days of being the world's economic basket case may soon be over.

ACKNOWLEDGMENTS

COLLEAGUES IN THE NATIONAL BUREAU of Economic Research's Africa Group provided useful reactions on an early version of the opening essay at a February 2008 conference. Special thanks go to David Weil, the group's organizer, and to Olu Ajakaiye, Bill Easterly, Rachel Glennerster, and Isaac Mbiti for their detailed comments during and following that meeting. I received superb research assistance from Sarath Sanga, Pamela Sud, and especially Melanie Wasserman, who helped assemble the data and create the figures and also provided useful comments on the text.

I am indebted to Ray Fisman, my co-author on another book (*Economic Gangsters: Corruption, Violence and the Poverty of Nations*,

Princeton University Press), where several related arguments are also made, especially the discussions of climate, conflict, the rapid conflict prevention support mechanism, and the promise randomized evaluations hold in development. I'd also like to thank my collaborators John Bellows, Chris Blattman, John Dykema, Rachel Glennerster, Melissa Gonzalez-Brenes, Shanker Satyanath, Ernest Sergenti, Kate Whiteside, Yongmei Zhou, and Alix Zwane. I'd especially like to thank Michael Kremer, for giving me my first fieldwork opportunity in Kenya back in 1997, and for his intellectual inspiration and friendship ever since. During that summer and my next few stints in Busia, I was blessed to work with Chip Bury, Mary Kay Gugerty, Sylvie Moulin, Robert Namunyu, Susan Walji, Polycarp Waswa, and Maureen Wechuli, who provided constant insight into life in rural Kenya.

While they are too numerous to name individually here, I could never have written this book without my colleagues in the U.C. Berkeley Economics Department, Agricultural and Resource Economics Department, Center for African Studies, and Center of Evaluation for Global Action (CEGA), and at Stanford's Center for International Development, where I wrote the *Boston Review* article in early 2008 while on sabbatical leave from Berkeley.

This book builds on over a decade of academic research on African economic and political development, which was made possible by generous financial support from the U.S. National Science Foundation, National Institutes of Health, the Bill and Melinda Gates Foundation, google.org, the World Bank, Social Science Research Council, the Sloan Foundation, the Harry F. Guggenheim Foundation, International Child Support (ICS), the Meatu Tanzania District Council, and the University of California, Berkeley Committee on Research and Center for Health Research, among others.

EDWARD MIGUEL

This year my wife Ali and I have been blessed with a darling son, Elias, the most precious little boy in the whole world. I dedicate this book to him.

APPENDIX OF RESOURCES

SOME OF THE BEST-KNOWN ACADEMIC work that speaks to the debate on African economic development includes Daron Acemoglu, James Robinson and Simon Johnson (2001), "The Colonial Origins of Comparative Development: An Empirical Investigation," *American Economic Review*; Robert Bates (1981), *Markets and States in Tropical Africa*, University of California Press; Paul Collier and Jan Gunning (1999), "Explaining African Economic Performance," *Journal of Economic Literature*; William Easterly and Ross Levine (1997), "Africa's Growth Tragedy: Policies and Ethnic Divisions," *Quarterly Journal of Economics*; Jeffrey Herbst (2000), *States and Power in Africa: Comparative Lessons in Authority and Control*, Princeton University Press; and Jeffrey Sachs and Andrew Warner (1997), "Sources of Slow Growth in African Economies," *Journal of African Economies*.

Several insightful World Bank publications discuss Africa's recent economic growth. These include: *Recent Economic Performance in Sub-Saharan Africa*, AFRCE, April 12, 2006; *Accelerating Development Outcomes in Africa: Progress and Change in the Africa Action Plan*, Development Committee, April 15, 2007; Benno Ndulu (with Lopamudra Chakraborti, Lebohang Lijane, Vijaya Ramachandran, and Jerome Wolgin) (2007), *Challenges of African Growth: Opportunities, Constraints and Strategic Decisions*; and Harry G. Broadman (with Gozde Isik, Sonia Plaza, Xiaoqing Ye, and Yutaka Yoshino) (2007), *Africa's Silk Road: China and India's New Economic Frontier*.

Oil prices can be found on the Energy Information Administration Web site at http://tonto.eia.doe.gov/dnav/pet/hist/wtotworldw.htm; copper prices on the New York Mercantile Exchange website: http://www.nymex.com/cop_fut_histspot.aspx; and coffee prices on the International Coffee Organization website: http://www.ico.org/asp/select10.asp.

For a theoretical discussion of how economic growth in China and India could affect long-run prospects in Africa, see Marcos Chamon and Michael Kremer (2006), "Asian Growth and African Development" in the *American Economic Association Papers and Proceedings*.

For a fascinating discussion of how telecommunications technology is affecting African economies, see Jenny Aker, "Does Digital Provide or Divide? The Impact of Cell Phones on Grain Markets in Niger," unpublished working paper University of California, Berkeley.

A recent article contains interesting interviews with Chinese investors in Africa: Howard W. French and Lydia Polgreen, "Entrepreneurs From China Flourish in Africa," *New York Times*, August 18, 2007. Another nice reference on Chinese influence in Africa is Lydia Polgreen and Howard W. French, "China's Trade in Africa Carries a Price Tag," *New York Times*, August 21, 2007.

Ray Fisman makes a related point about how Western sanctions may strengthen Chinese bargaining power in Sudan in "Diamonds are a Guerrilla's Best Friend," *Slate*, August 17, 2007.

An influential reference on the global implications of U.S. cotton subsidies is Oxfam's 2002 Briefing Paper #30, "Cultivating Poverty: The Impact of U.S. Cotton Subsidies on Africa."

For discussion of foreign aid, refer to Jeffrey

Sachs (2005), *The End of Poverty: Economic Possibilities for Our Time*, Penguin Press; and William Easterly (2006), *The White Man's Burden: Why the West's Efforts to Aid the Rest Have Done So Much Ill and So Little Good*, Penguin Press. Other important contributions in this vast literature include William Easterly, (2003) "Can Foreign Aid Buy Growth?" *Journal of Economic Perspectives*; and Adam Przeworski and James R. Vreeland (2000) "The impact of IMG programs on economic growth," *Journal of Development Economics*. Figure 2 in Easterly (2003) clearly illustrates the sharp drop-off in foreign aid at the Cold War's end.

The International Peace Research Institute of Oslo (PRIO) / Uppsala Armed Conflict Database contains the most widely used measures of global armed conflict.

Two recent research papers on post-war legacies are Christopher Blattman (2007), "From

Violence to Voting: War and political participation in Uganda," manuscript, Yale University; and John Bellows and Edward Miguel (2008), "War and Local Collective Action in Sierra Leone," manuscript, University of California, Berkeley.

For the research on economic shocks and civil war, refer to the research papers: Edward Miguel, Shanker Satyanath, and Ernest Sergenti (2004), "Economic Shocks and Civil Conflict: An Instrumental Variables Approach," *Journal of Political Economy*; and Markus Bruckner and Antonio Ciccone (2007), "Growth, Democracy, and Civil War," manuscript, Universitat Pompeu Fabra.

For further work describing the "rapid conflict prevention support" proposal, see my articles "Poverty and Violence: An Overview of Recent Research and Implications for Foreign Aid," in (2007) *Too Poor for Peace? Global Poverty,*

Conflict and Security in the 21st Century, (eds.) Lael Brainard and Derek Chollet, Brookings Institution Press; and "Stop Conflict Before it Starts," *Business Week*, September 18, 2006. RCPS is laid out in greater detail in my 2008 book with Ray Fisman, *Economic Gangsters: Corruption, Violence, and the Poverty of Nations* (Princeton University Press).

For more information on Botswana's drought-relief program, refer to Theodore Valentine (1993), "Drought, Transfers, Entitlements and Income Distribution: The Botswana Experience," *World Development* 21, no. 1: pp. 109–26.

I had a conversation with President Masire about the drought-relief program on August 2, 2006 in Aspen, Colorado, at the Brookings-Blum Roundtable examining "The Tangled Web: Breaking the Poverty-Insecurity Nexus."

The International Energy Agency Statistics, 2007 (http://www.iea.org) contains detailed global data on CO_2 emissions.

The predicted temperature changes mentioned in the text are for the range of low-emissions to high-emissions scenarios described in the 2007 IPCC Report: see http://www.ipcc.ch/ipccreports/assessments-reports.htm/AR4WG1_Pub_SPM-v2.pdf, p. 13.

The discussion of climate change in the Sahel is based on my ongoing research with John Dykema of Harvard University and Shanker Satyanath and Ernest Sergenti of New York University. There is no single accepted definition of the Sahel. The following organizations have different definitions: USAID (http://www.usaid.gov/press/factsheets/2005/fs050803.html), the Community of Sahel-Saharan States (http://www.africa-union.org/root/au/RECs/cen_sad.htm), and the

International Development Research Centre (http://www.idrc.ca/en/ev-43109-201-1-DO_TOPIC.html). A reasonable definition of the Sahel includes parts of the following fifteen countries: Burkina Faso, Cape Verde, Chad, Djibouti, Eritrea, Ethiopia, Gambia, Guinea-Bissau, Mali, Mauritania, Niger, Nigeria, Senegal, Somalia, and Sudan. The climate estimates for the Sahel come from a convenient geographic rectangle bounded between 4-25° North latitude and 13° West and 17° East longitude. The per-capita GDP figure in the text is population-weighted for these countries (minus Somalia, which has no reliable national income figures for recent years) and comes from the World Development Indicators (http://devdata.worldbank.org/wdi2006/contents/cover.htm). Income is not adjusted for purchasing power.

For a fascinating account of the violent suppression of the Mau Mau uprising in late colonial Kenya, see David M. Anderson (2005), *Histories of the Hanged: The Dirty War in Kenya and the End of Empire*, W.W. Norton and Company.

For more on Latin America's tumultuous post-independence era, see Chris Leuchars (2002), *To the Bitter End: Paraguay and the War of the Triple Alliance*, Greenwood Publishing. For a comparison of post-independence Latin America and Africa, refer to Robert Bates, John H. Coatsworth, and Jeffrey G. Williamson (2006), "Lost Decades: Lessons from Post-Independence Latin America for Today's Africa," National Bureau of Economic Research Working Paper #12610.

For a discussion of the financial settlement for Kenyan torture victims, refer to "Kenyans to Pay for the Sin of Detention," *Daily Nation*, August 30, 2008. Note that Kenya's Freedom House score has dropped from a 3 to a 4 in

2008, indicating less democracy. This likely reflects the stolen December 2007 election rather than the more recent democratic consolidation, power-sharing deal, and other reforms described in the text.

The source of the Nairobi Stock Exchange information is *DataServe*.

Clark Gibson of the University of California, San Diego and co-authors have assembled persuasive statistical evidence on the extent of vote rigging in the December 2007 Kenyan elections by comparing large-scale exit-poll data to official vote returns.

I have been delighted that some in the mainstream media now also believe Africa might be at a turning point. Roger Cohen has recently written on related issues in *The New York Times*, in his August 20, 2008 column "News Good Enough to Bury."

The research paper that finds a strong link between proximity to competitive elections and stronger ethnic identities is Benn Eifert, Edward Miguel, and Daniel Posner (2008), "Political Identification and Ethnic Identification in Africa," unpublished manuscript, University of California, Berkeley and University of California, Los Angeles.

The discussion of how Asian trade and aid ties affect African institutions is Erik Meyersson, Gerard Padro-i-Miquel, and Nancy Qian (2008), "The Rise of China and the Natural Resource Curse in Africa," unpublished working paper, Brown University and London School of Economics.

Readers interested in the randomized evaluation methodology should refer to Esther Duflo, Michael Kremer, and Rachel Glennerster's (2008) *Handbook of Development Economics* chapter "Using Randomization in Development Economics Research: A Toolkit" for a detailed discussion of the method, as well as a discussion of seminal randomized experimental studies within economics, including Robert J. Lalonde's (1986) piece "Evaluating the Econometric Evaluations of Training Programs Using Experimental Data," *American Economic Review*, 76(4), pp. 602-620. The Mexican *Progresa* program was a pioneering use of randomized evaluation within development economics; see T. Paul Schultz (2004), "School subsidies for the poor: evaluating the Mexican *Progresa* Poverty Program," *Journal of Development Economics*, 74(1), pp. 199-250.

Kremer and Miguel's main nonprofit collaborators are currently: Innovations for Poverty Action (http://www.poverty-action.org/) the MIT J-PAL (http://www.povertylab.com/), and the Berkeley CEGA (http://cega.berkeley.edu/).

The academic paper on deworming is Edward

Miguel and Michael Kremer (2004), "Worms: Identifying Impacts on Education and Health in the Presence of Treatment Externalities," *Econometrica*, 72(1), pp. 159-217. This and the other Busia studies can also be found on the J-PAL website.

Researchers in Busia have also recently used randomized evaluation to assess which types of sex-education lessons are most effective in preventing pregnancy and sexually transmitted diseases among young African schoolgirls. In case you're wondering, traditional sex education doesn't reduce unsafe sex, but targeted lessons warning girls about older "sugar daddies" do. See Pascaline Dupas (2006), "Relative Risks and the Market for Sex: Teenagers, Sugar Daddies, and HIV in Kenya," unpublished working paper, Dartmouth College; and Esther Duflo, Pascaline Dupas, Michael Kremer, and Samuel Sinei, "Education and HIV/AIDS Prevention: Evidence from a randomized evaluation in Western Kenya," World Bank Policy Research Working Paper #4024, June 2006.

For information on deworming in Ghana, refer to UNICEF press release, "4.5 million children across Ghana to be dewormed," February 5, 2007.

The best reference on how randomized evaluations can be used to understand which policies can reduce corruption and improve governance is Ben Olken (2007), "Monitoring Corruption: Evidence from a Field Experiment in Indonesia," *Journal of Political Economy*, 115(2), pp. 200-249.

Maintaining the highest ethical standards is a very important issue for impact evaluations. All academic research projects involving human subjects must be approved by a university's institutional review board to ensure that the ethical lapses of the past are not repeated today. All of the Busia projects described above, as well as the Olken study, underwent such a review.

ABOUT THE CONTRIBUTORS

EDWARD MIGUEL is Associate Professor of Economics at the University of California, Berkeley and coauthor with Ray Fisman of *Economic Gangsters: Corruption, Violence, and the Poverty of Nations.*

OLU AJAKAIYE is Research Director at the African Economic Research Consortium.

KEN BANKS has spent the last fifteen years working on projects in Africa and is the founder of kiwanja.net. He divides his time between Cambridge and Stanford University.

Robert H. Bates, Eaton Professor of the Science of Government at Harvard University, is co-author and co-editor of *The Political Economy of Economic Growth in Africa*, 1960-2000 and *When Things Fell Apart: State Failure in Late-Century Africa*.

Paul Collier is Professor of Economics at Oxford University and Director of the Oxford Center for the Study of African Economies. His book *The Bottom Billion* won the 2008 Lionel Gelber Prize.

Rachel Glennerster is Executive Director of the Abdul Latif Jameel Poverty Action Lab at the Massachusetts Institute of Technology.

Rosamond Naylor is Senior Fellow at the Freeman Spogli Institute for International Studies and the Woods Institute for the Environment at Stanford University. She is Director of the Program on Food Security and the Environment.

SMITA SINGH is Director of the Global Development Program at The William and Flora Hewlett Foundation.

DAVID N. WEIL is Professor of Economics at Brown University and Research Associate of the National Bureau of Economic Research (NBER). He is co-director of the NBER project on African development success.

JEREMY M. WEINSTEIN, Assistant Professor of Political Science and Director of the Center for African Studies at Stanford University, is author of *Inside Rebellion: The Politics of Insurgent Violence*.

BOSTON REVIEW BOOKS

Boston Review Books are accessible, short books that take ideas seriously. They are animated by hope, committed to equality, and convinced that the imagination eludes political categories. The editors aim to establish a public space in which people can loosen the hold of conventional preconceptions and start to reason together across the lines others are so busily drawing.

The Men in My Life   VIVIAN GORNICK

Inventing American History   WILLIAM HOGELAND

Africa's Turn?   EDWARD MIGUEL